One Degree West

First Series: Creative Nonfiction

Julene Bair

To Helen and Bruce,
In hopes that some-
thing of my wheat
farming stories
speaks to your
experiences on the
high plains of Canada.
Julene Bair

ONE DEGREE WEST

Reflections of a Plainsdaughter

Mid-List Press
Minneapolis

Manufactured in the United States of America
Mid-List Press, 4324 12th Avenue South, Minneapolis, MN 55407-3218
Web site address: www.midlist.org

ISBN: 0-92281145-8
First printing: March 2000
05   04   03   02   00   5   4   3   2   1

Cover and text design: Lane Stiles

The following essays appeared earlier in different forms: "At Forty-five" in *The Chicago Tribune Sunday Magazine*; "Beacons" in *Single Mother's Companion*, ed. Marsha R. Leslie (Seattle: Seal Press, 1994); "Disappearances" (as "Thanksgiving on the Plains") in *Iowa Woman*; "The Gleaners" and "Inside Spaces" in *Northern Lights*; "Housewives, Fieldhusbands" in *Connecting: Twenty Prominent Authors Write about the Relationships that Shape Our Lives*, ed. Lee Gutkind (New York: Tarcher, 1998); "Reaching Down" in *Fourth Genre*, Volume 1, Number 1, 1999, published by Michigan State University Press.

♾ The paper used in this publication meets the minimum requirements of the American National Standard for Information Sciences—Permanence of Paper for Printed Library Materials, ANSI Z39.48-1984.

To my parents, Harold and Jasmin

When we examine a nest,
we place ourselves at the origin of confidence in the world.

—Gaston Bachelard, The Poetics of Space

Contents

Disappearances

          I grew up on the mild-green, short-tufted buffalo grass prairies of northwestern Kansas. The High Plains they are called, and my family's spot upon them was Highland Farm. We were lifted on that great plain, four thousand feet above sea level, exposed to the sky, not cradled and protected by the earth the way Iowa or Minnesota farm families are. Each family in rural Kansas was alone together on the flat. At night we had distant yellow lights to remind us that we did have neighbors, but when those blinked off at bedtime, only the moon and stars penetrated the dark. Coyotes howled in our front yard.

          When the Thanksgiving season approaches, I think of that home place and our big corner of Kansas more intensely than at other times, though, to tell the truth, it is on my mind always. Our rock-hard farmyard, gnarly with implement tracks and bony bumps, is the ground I walk on still, the given against which the baseline of my city life is too many eons removed. Here in town, the earth suffocates beneath pavement. Reality seems smoothed over, and I feel as if I'm the only one who isn't fooled. Beneath sidewalks and somehow beyond my neighbors' shiny cars and their meticulously raked yards, and then at whichever friend's house my son and I dine this year, a wintry defiance lurks, reminding me that except for that one savory hour when we eat, this holiday is a heart beating out into nothingness.

          Thanksgiving, that day when we feasted on the bounty of our work, was often a forlorn holiday in Kansas. The hour at table was joyous, but the season itself boded emptiness and decline. This was especially true when we traveled. I have visions of desolate blacktops, straight and narrow between flat fields of stubble. The destinations were always towns where widowed great-aunts lived, their nondescript Plymouths parked in the unpaved drives of their trailer houses. Wandering the foreign burg with a remote cousin, I would try to imagine glamour in the unfamiliar surroundings despite streets of inelegant frozen mud. The movie theater, if there was one, would be shuttered, and the only traffic would be a sedate dirty pickup, jiggling slowly over the ruts as a farmer, with his belly full of food and relatives, headed out to a pasture to check his livestock.

The high point of those Thanksgivings came for me once when my brother Clark, home from his first teaching job in the far-off, eastern part of the state, let me drive his black GTO the entire hundred miles from our farm to Aunt Rosie's. I aimed the car with earnest precision, filling with pride as Clark complimented me. "Wow! You're a natural!"

I stared at my brother for as long as my fear of going off the road would allow. "You're just saying that, aren't you?"

"No! I mean it. If I didn't know better, I'd think you'd been driving since you were ten."

My brothers were that age when they started driving the pickup around the farm, but now Dad told me I would have to wait until there was a "teen" in my age, which wouldn't be until the following May.

Clark had graduated high school when I was only nine. He came home less and less frequently as the years passed, his departure merely the first of many disappearances I would witness. Thirty years later, he would be killed in a bicycling accident on Highway One, in California. "So far afield," I wrote in a memorial piece a year or so after the funeral, and my mother, who tends to hold her emotions close, confessed that those words caused her to set the article down and cry. We kids always took it for granted that to leave Kansas was a good thing.

Thanksgivings at home were more fun, although the guests delayed their arrival to the last anguished minute. The smell of roasting turkey reached into the farthest corners of the house, and my brother Bruce, five years my elder, became bored enough to play with me. He would challenge me to a contest I was sure to lose, such as seeing how far we could skate in our stockinged feet down the planks in the fake wood grain linoleum our mother had waxed the day before. Promptly yelled at, we would then loll in the easy chairs beside the windows at the far end of the big dining room. I would try to concentrate on a book, but my hair caught electricity from the vinyl recliner, and a menacing ionic charge hovered between Bruce and me as well. I could tell when his boredom was about to erupt in scathing sarcasm. The only potential victim in the vicinity, I would flee out into the frost-killed forest of my mother's yard. I bounced a stick along the sidewalk, stooped to cuddle a cat or dog, or went down to the barn to stroke the neck of Queenie, my ill-tempered mare. Sparks and dust would shoot up from her roan coat, thick for winter, causing her to lay her ears back and turn her rump on me. I would wander the back lot near the windbreak and climb around on ancient combines and in rusted truck cabs until finally I heard cars pulling into the yard.

The day was transformed. My girl cousins and I would dart back and forth among our aunts and uncles, swiping all the olives and sweet pickles off the relish tray. After the meal, we would tiptoe behind the barn and slide the door shut before Queenie made a dash for it. I would jam the cold bit into her mouth, then lead her out the front door and over to the abandoned concrete stock tank, where each cousin would perch in turn. After many attempts, we usually managed to get Queenie positioned right and steadied long enough for all to get aboard. We would ride out beyond the windbreak. Once, when a pheasant squawked and burst from the stubble, Queenie saw her chance and shied. My cousins and I, still holding onto one another, flew off. I clung to the reins, which jerked us around in an arc and thudded us to the ground beneath the mare's front feet. Bruised in that exploit, we all four grabbed shovels and went to work on the anthill out by the storm cellar. We dug out of scientific interest in hibernation, we explained to our parents, but really it was out of a will to wreak vengeance on the animal kingdom, no matter how far down the ladder we had to stoop.

Even though I grew drunk with companionship on those rare Thanksgiving afternoons, dark would fall inevitably and the cousins would leave. The next morning the long weekend would begin. A thousand ewes chomped ensilage in the corrals, but the place seemed empty to me.

Our way of life was dying. I sensed this even then. Only old people lived in the fifty houses in my great-aunts' towns. Nearer home, a crop of widows and divorcees—my parents' sisters—began migrating, with my cousins, to Colorado cities. My brother Bruce and I departed as Clark had done, when we graduated high school. Today only my father and one of his Colorado-dwelling sisters still own farms. No one in my generation works the land. Some of us have tried our hands at farming, but generally only when other options have fallen through. I, for instance, went back to the farm at thirty-five, pregnant, and broke after a failed marriage. The return was humiliating, but soon the Kansas elements reclaimed me. Having been reared in the harsh environment, I hadn't felt truly alive since I last battled dirt and wind. That first spring, I rejoiced in the texture of the earth behind the plow. In the shop, armed with a grease gun, I scooted on a dolly beneath tractors, soothed by the smell of dust and grease, and by the massive machinery.

I reveled in its power. Ancestors only a couple generations before me had made their tenuous claim on the prairie, and now we were thundering over it in tractors bigger than their houses. But there were fewer of us. My parents, like so many farmers, had moved to town many years before, trading the farm I had grown up on for land closer to their other holdings. Children had spilled out of my grandparents' sod shanties; now I was living alone on this other ground, in a two-story, four-bedroom house with one baby boy. My parents thought I was crazy to want to live, as Mom said, "out in the middle of nowhere like that, in that ramshackle house." Dad commuted to this farm as if it were a factory, the land suited only for the mass production of crops, no longer a place to live.

The prairie of my childhood, with its cloud-shadowed rises and mild ravines, had disappeared. Instead of buffalo grass, rows of irrigated corn and soybeans vee-d into the distances. The state's floral pride, the sunflower, wasn't prominent along roadsides anymore, where only the toughest grasses survived the many poisons. When I walked through ditches on my way from the pickup to a waiting tractor, no grasshoppers clacked aloft to startle me. As a child, I had grown oblivious to their landings on my breastbone. The snake population had diminished as well, making such treks across ditches less foolhardy, but I missed the edge of adventure in the landscape.

Denuded of snakes and cousins, of friends, life in Kansas was even lonelier than in childhood. After two years, I began to make plans for my second migration.

The last Thanksgiving dinner I had in Kansas was at my parents' house. My son Jake and I were the only guests. My brother Bruce, although he was writing for a newspaper in another Kansas town, had taken his family to Arkansas to see his wife's parents. Clark was teaching chemistry at a junior college in Chico, California, too far to travel for a brief visit. There were no aunts and uncles around anymore. My mother and I went through the motions—stuffed the turkey, baked the pies, even got out the good china. But after we had loaded the dishwasher, put the tinfoil over the turkey and packaged up my share of leftovers, Mom went off to join Dad for a nap, and I, glad to have the event over with, plunked Jake into his car seat and started back to the farm.

The southerly sun cast angled light over miles of stubble—wheat, corn, and sorghum. Harvest had been laid up in the fat corrugated grain bins on the farms, and the sun made the elevators—twin white towers in every town—glisten. Jake fell asleep, and once home, I carried him inside and laid him in his crib. The house was silent, grown dingy in our absence. To off-set the loneliness, I sat down in the kitchen and ate another piece of pecan pie. Then, stuffed beyond belief, I pulled on my farmer's flannel-lined denim jacket and went outside into the falling evening to walk. I followed the ruts the combine and trucks had torn through the yard after an early snow, which had frustrated our corn harvest. The shop's wide doorway gaped black and quiet where the day before my father's hammer had clanged, realigning a bent sweep rod beneath the flame of his acetylene torch.

I strolled among the grain bins, some squat, some tall, all of them full. At the bases of their doors lay mounds of grain that had escaped through the cracks. When I came to the largest bin, I stretched out my arms to embrace it and lay my cheek against the cold tin hillocks. Back in July I had waded this wheat in the beds of trucks, holding my scoop out to direct its flow from the combine augers. Yet in the harvest rush, I'd forgotten to capture a bag full before we dusted the crop with Malathion and binned it. Beneath the metal lay twenty thousand bushels of wheat, and Mom had baked her Thanksgiving bread with white flour from the store. With winter coming and Jake asleep in the quiet house, all that bounty seemed sterile and useless, the future hol-low. I asked myself the question my father has obsessed on ever since his boys left for other occupations: *Who will carry on?*

Julene and her son Jake, he came to think during the two years we lived there. I relished my stature in the wake of my broth-ers' defections. I wanted Jake and me to be his answer, but had come, finally, to the disappointing conclusion that we were not.

Today, I live eight hundred miles from western Kansas, too far to travel for brief holiday breaks, but I've returned for the past four summers. I want my son to know his grandparents and their land. I can't uproot myself completely, nor reconcile myself to the fact that the land, once lost to me, then briefly reclaimed, is not our future.

Summers are always a busy time in Kansas, as long as it hasn't hailed or come a severe drought. Wheat trucks barrel down the gravel roads in July, hauling their bounty to the elevators, then, rattling empty, careen back to the fields, where the combines graze like giant mantises. I like to see the wheat before the machines pull in, a county full of it. I like to walk in it when it is unscathed and trackless, its trillions of bristles whispering. The effect is delusory, as if the occurrence of so much grain in one place is a natural phenomenon, and walking in it, I am in communion with a natural element, as ubiquitous as air or water or heat.

It was on a day like that a couple summers ago, when the buds were burnished gold but the stalks still too green to cut, that I decided to pay a visit to the home place. The road carried me out there, past both abandoned and still vital farmsteads, where green combines and red and white trucks waited silent and ready, the sun glinting off their windshields. On the sole curve, past the Rickard place, I felt the excitement in my belly from when I was a kid driving home from high school and would take the turn too fast. I drove with my windows down, the air rushing in, fire-lapped and dry. Fifteen miles of that, the tires rumbling over gravel, an occasional rock dinging the tailpipe, and then there it was, still five miles away, but prominently visible because of the gentle rise on which it stood. The Carlson farmstead was my family's center of gravity, but others could drive right by it, not even feeling the magnet's pull in their stomachs, as someone in a wheat truck did just then, filling the car with dust. I swerved and re-fastened my attention to the road until I arrived at the turn onto the half-mile of dirt track. After a dip between what used to be two pastures, but were now wheat fields, the trail dead-ended in our old farmyard.

I parked below the knoll leading up to the house. Opening

the car door onto what I expected to be mere heat and wind, I was startled by a deer with a huge crest of antlers. It tore out of the thicket that had once been our north yard, where Dad had braced up the cherry tree with a makeshift post and rail crutch, and leapt past the remnants of the sheep barn into the wheat field. The pasture beyond that long building had once seemed to reach into eternity, but was now reduced to a single circle of wheat beneath the breadth of a pivot sprinkler. I watched the deer bound through the wheat like a merry-go-round animal, his rack aligned in the crosshairs of the vacant afternoon, then turned back to the house yard.

Some of my mother's yellow rosebushes were in bloom, and I imagined her posing before them, as she had for one of the pictures in the family photo album, the skirt of her house-dress hugging her belly and thighs in the wind, which was always too intense and bothersome—full of dust in summer and needling cold in winter—to be called a breeze. I walked carefully, pulling back the branches that had overgrown the sidewalk, trying not to break or trample anything that would make the deer's haven less familiar when he returned. Millions of moments circled inside me, stirred by this visit as were the leaves overhead, tossed by the perennial wind. Should I tell Mom about the deer and the flowers, I wondered? She would be pleased to hear about them, but reminding her of the empty house would upset her. She never would have agreed to the trade, she once told me, had she known the farmstead her father built would wind up abandoned.

Grand by local standards, the old house is a monument to our dead: Grandpa Carlson, with his bald head, his Swedish accent and his way of turning big dreams into reality; Grandma Carlson with her nubbin bun, her sternness and her complaining; Uncle John, the farming hope of my mother's family, who was struck by lightning while driving a tractor; and now Clark, my older brother, who had died just the previous year. It was his death, so recent, that brought me to the home place that day.

Someone planted two evergreen trees after we moved. I had to lift their branches to make my way up the wide steps of the south porch. I ran my hand down the beveled glass in the front entry, then discovered the door unlocked. The house was as cold as a walk-in meat locker, holding the chill over from the night. Glass still lined the sashes of the bay windows, some of it original, rippled, hand-blown—a wonder, since the Carlsons, then the Bairs had raised children in the house, and at least two other families had lived in it since we left. I had forgotten how big the windows were. No easy chairs beckoned from in front of them, however, and the air conditioner had been removed from below the middle one, leaving a hole that framed a square patch of brush. Someone had torn the wall out between the dining room and Mom's sewing room. They laid a turquoise carpet over the wood grain linoleum Bruce and I had skated down. During my long absence, the house had been restored in my mind to its original elegance, so I was disappointed all over again by the north wall, which separated the dining room from the kitchen. Originally, a set of leaded glass cabinets and a mantel with a mirror above it appointed that wall, but, saying these features were too old to repair, my parents had them torn out the same year they had the upstairs balcony removed.

My mother had hung Clark's senior picture in the middle of the wall, when it was newly blank. As a child, I stared at the picture often and proudly, noticing how perfectly squared were his shoulders, the bows of his tie and his flattop. Remembering that picture's isolation reminded me of the time his classmates went on a field trip to Colorado Springs and Dad made Clark stay home to help with lambing season, and another time when he dressed up in the same gray suit he wore in the picture, to compete in a high school best-groomed contest. He wasn't able to get the grease out from under his fingernails, had even tried gas, and then reeked of the fumes. I remembered him standing in the dining room beside the varnished pine door leading onto the mud porch, where he'd scrubbed for nearly an hour. He let

Mom perfect his tie knot, then said, his eyes brimming, "I look like a dumb farmer."

Upstairs, the hallway was still fifteen feet wide. Mom and Dad's room, gaping and bedless, no longer exuded mystery. Mom had always kept the curtains drawn over the windows, making it darker than the rest of the house. My cousins and I once got in trouble for sneaking into the room at night when the adults were gathered in the living room below. We tried on Mom's costume jewelry and wobbled in her heels before her big round dresser mirror.

Bruce's room had one window, looking west over the backyard. When as a child I entered his messy lair, through the narrow corridor walling off the stairwell, the afternoon light exploded through that window, and it seemed as if Bruce lived in the most spacious room of all. I now leaned my forehead against the filmy pane and looked down into the backyard. Concealed in the plum and olive thicket, I knew, was a concrete dome with a rusted vent pipe sticking up in the middle—the cap over the septic tank. To me as a child, it had been a mysterious surface on which to prance. There was no odor, just the bewitching contour of a spaceship. I would sit on it early evenings and watch the sky blaze over the elm windbreak beyond the hog lot. During fall sunsets, it was as if the yard's bare limbs were strewn with a giant canopy of rainbow satin. I would watch until I could barely distinguish the outline of the tall, ark-shaped hog feeder beyond the wire fence.

My mother told me that her older siblings had grown up in a sod house near the spot where the feeder now stood, but the roof had blown off and the blocks were crumbling by the time she was born. I would sit until she called me in to help serve supper at the big Formica dining table, where waited my father, two or three hired men, and my brothers, whose work among the men I envied.

I turned and leaned on my brother Bruce's sill. His room

was bare now, like all the others, but had once contained two floor-to-ceiling stacks of cigar boxes filled with things I was afraid to sneak peeks at as a girl. I feared he may have tied an invisible thread between the dresser and his blue-painted chest of drawers or come up with some other devious detection system and would then repay me for the trespass. He collected arrowheads, animal teeth, sulfur for stink bombs, bullet casings, bird bones, bug carcasses, gunpowder gleaned from spent firecrackers, and chunks of molten glass he'd found in our dump, a bulldozed hole south of the house. He had slithered about the farmstead, making discoveries on his own ever since he was a toddler, sparking proud wonder in our parents, who were impressed by his curiosity and genius. And then I had come along, diverting some—but nowhere near enough, I had always felt—of their attention. I followed him everywhere in the manner of a younger sibling, trying to share in his discoveries, trying to win his admiration, while he fended me off with insults and made it clear he wished I would evaporate.

A different dynamic was at work between him and Clark. Bruce out-charmed his brother, whose temperament, as the eldest child, was serious, sensitive, and eager. While our father held Clark up to the First National Bank calendar and taught him his numbers when he was only three, then taught him to spell the word "International" by pointing out the letters on a wheat truck dashboard, Bruce engineered his own education. He found arrowheads on pasture hills, built a raft on which he attempted to float the Republican River (but wound up sinking), and subscribed to the Junior Audubon Society. He was the only one among us who knew there was no such thing as a chicken hawk. The hawks we referred to in that way were sometimes red-tails, sometimes ferruginous, he replied without hesitation when, a decade into adulthood, I developed my own interest in birds.

I crossed the hallway and paused for a moment before entering Clark's room. I wished there were some ritual by which

I could make his ghost appear, some means to convince myself he still existed. The frequent dreams I had about him were not enough. I crossed the threshold and blew a kiss onto the air where his tin-framed bed used to be. During my early childhood, when Clark was a teenager, his room had radiated brains and accomplishment. His grand prize 4-H ribbons, for bottle calves, lambs and for test plots of wheat, had hung beside his Future Farmer of America and honor roll certificates. I walked to his window. He had stared out at the same baked gray farmyard as I had, with the big barn opposite and the dead cottonwood tree by the concrete stock tank where my cousins and I had mounted Queenie. The house stood at the center of Grandma Carlson's land, leased by our father, and when Clark got up mornings, he must have looked out to where his tractor waited for him in the nearest field. Behind it, a straight-edged line would have separated the dark dirt from the gray. He might have computed, on waking, as I did years later when I finally got my chance to farm, how many hours it would take him to finish the field. If he had any daylight left, he would use it to wash and polish his car, a red Ford Falcon. On Saturday nights, Dad let him fill it up from the farm gas tank, and he drove it to town, where, in the manner of kids all over the High Plains, he cruised Main Street in search of fellowship with his own kind.

At home, he played Connie Francis and Everly Brothers albums on his two-tone, vinyl-covered stereo with the fold-out speakers. Stereo was new then, and he was an aficionado, as he was of all technology. I associate my brother Clark with the Soviet satellite, Sputnik. We watched it together as a family the first night it passed over us, and Clark followed its arc every night thereafter. He spoke of the achievement with awe, and fear, not of what the Russians could do, but of what he might never get to do. He wanted to go to college and become a scientist, but there was always the danger that he might return home. Both boys received a mixed message from our compelling, charismatic, strong-willed father, who admired his sons' brains, but himself lived to farm. Either thing they chose, whether a career elsewhere or farming, would constitute failure, because each precluded the other.

Clark named our white tomcat Sputnik and hung wadded paper on a string from the dining room ceiling register. We would watch the cat bat the makeshift toy around for hours, Clark giggling "like a hyena," Mom accused. She didn't like her eldest's indelicate humor—his burps, his demonstrative laughter. She had too much invested in his perfection. I realize this because, as the mother of only one child, I struggle against investing even more such hope.

My parents gave Clark a telescope for Christmas when he was fourteen. It was a year when Dad got his way and we opened the presents on Christmas Eve. Mom had a Calvinist streak in her and believed that waiting until Christmas morning would make us more worthy and appreciative of our gifts.

We heard shouting after we had all, I thought, gone to bed. "Come here! Come here! I found it!"

"What's all the bellering about?" Mom said, fastening the rhinestone buttons on the new rose satin quilted robe Dad had given her. I trotted behind her and Dad down the stairs, through the dining room and mud porch, and out onto the east porch steps. Bruce slept on upstairs.

"I found Saturn!" Clark shouted.

"Good Lord," Mom said. "Have you been out here all this time? You'll freeze to death." But she bent over the eyepiece he held for her.

Clark ran the fingers of his free hand through his flattop as he waited for her to see.

"Where? I don't see anything."

Clark readjusted the scope for her, and she looked again. "Oh my," she said, forgetting for a moment to shiver. "That sure is something."

"I tell you," my father said, "if this son of yours uses even half his brains, those Russians won't stand a chance."

When he was seventeen, Clark taught me to jitterbug to Elvis Presley albums. "Toe-heel, toe-heel, back, toe-heel," he chanted, showing me the steps.

I stood on his bed to compensate for the height difference. "Twirl me," I begged. He sent me out to the ends of his long arms, spun me, and brought me back.

Mom shouted up the stairs for us to "watch out up there! You're going to cave the house in!"

Then he went away to college. I was supposed to be happy for him, and was, of course, because of his great accomplishment. He had graduated valedictorian from high school a year early. He had shown the town kids, and this after attending a one-room country school for his first eight grades. That school had been closed after my first year. I now rode the bus twenty miles to town. I too got good grades, and Clark, on his visits home, told me to study hard. I could be a scientist too. Like him.

When he died, he was forty-seven and I was thirty-nine. The sadness over losing him to his world was miniscule compared to his sudden and complete absence from all worlds. The finality of his death weighed the corners of my lips down in an expression that had been unfamiliar until then. This was not just sadness, but grief, my first complete lesson in it. The three-pointed constellation he had been part of, with Bruce and me, now sank below the horizon each night more quickly, without him at the top of it. Its three-dimensional shape had devolved into a mere line.

It seemed fitting, on this tour of the past, to save my room for last. Vacant like the others, it had been painted a rude aqua, though pink and blue ribbony things still swirled against a white background in the wallpapered closet. The only child with two windows, I had the influence of Clark's bleak easterly view as well as the romance of Mom's south yard, where her best irises grew and where the locust tree brushed the rails of the balcony. There had been a mockingbird who clacked angrily at us whenever we ran up and down the rickety planks. Out that window I had first heard coyotes yelp, up close. I had imagined a whole pickup full of children screaming.

        Standing in my room, looking east. We took life in this house our grandfather built for granted. Like most kids, we fought and didn't know we loved each other and felt sorry for ourselves and longed to escape, but our lives had a spiritual edge. The bleakness and the distances nurtured a psychic dimension. The sky, whether endless blue or roiling with thunderheads, dwarfed our vanity. At night, in the summer, Mom and Dad steadied us, each in turn as we reached the age for clinging to the front fence, our toes wedged in the wire. They told us in amazed tones what little they knew about the stars. Once we saw moving lights in the sky that no one could explain.

Now, staring at the miles of wheat where the immense fan of buffalo grass had once opened onto sky, I reflected on how ironic it was that our migration to the cities had not diminished our impact on the land. With the aid of machinery and chemicals, and with families a tenth of their former size, we conquered the Plains, not just out of greed, but out of a failure to recognize what we loved and that love was reason enough not to destroy. Unable to fill the Plains with people, we settled for writing our name onto every inch of them, lest we forget ourselves and succumb to the spiritual vastness. Our farm once seemed infinite and painfully empty, whereas today even the world has limits. Were I to visit the house at night, I could now track dozens of satellites in the sky overhead. With this technology, we photograph the globe whole, the daytime shots optimistic with blue oceans, green prairies, a swirl of delicate clouds. But night shots reveal the glitter of manmade lights, blue-white fire along seacoasts encroaching inland—my aunts, my cousins, my brothers, and I folding back on ourselves, devouring.

I went outside and leaned on the gate post of the south yard, facing into the wind and the billowing wheat. Two kingbirds dove and chattered at me, their bellies yellow as sunflower petals. Most likely, they were direct descendants of the pair who had nested in the locust during my childhood. I scanned the branches overhead. My whole life, it had been this tree I imagined whenever I heard "Rock-a-bye Baby"—*Rock-a-bye baby, in the treetop. When the wind blows, the cradle will rock. When the bough breaks....* It had been this tree I thought of when Clark died. I had imagined a giant portion of it severed, as if by lightning. But the tree was thriving. The wind still gushed in its leaves. Its flat pods still rattled. On the outer reaches of a southern branch a nest bobbed, framed in blue. Fuzzy heads peeked over its edge.

I walked toward the old shop. Red ants toiled over the ground near the corner of the storm cellar, toting tiny pebbles of rose and white quartz up their immense mound. Although much larger, this had to be the same hill whose residents my cousins and I had tormented that Thanksgiving all those years before. Clark sat on the hill when he was two, a story Mom told just the previous Christmas, her eyes damp from both laughter and her loss, and from his pain, which she remembered as if it were her own.

Although I was home again last summer, I didn't go back out to the old place. I prefer remembering it when we lived there, as I have found myself doing more and more often this fall, as the air grows crisp, and the somberness looms. This Thanksgiving I'll spend in the city, where, like the ground, my ties seem smoothed over, my present unruffled. There will be an afternoon of companionship with colleagues who, like me, have no history here. The kingbirds will spend the day in Texas, or wherever it is they migrate winters. Some fall, after all the field work is done, the farmer who owns our old farmstead will throw one end of a log chain around the locust tree, loop the other end over his tractor hitch, and pull the birds' home down. He'll soak some rags in diesel fuel and set fire to ours.

I prefer envisioning a natural, or supernatural, combustion—lightning or the light of stars magnified—but I am jumping ahead, I guess, to the final verdict, when the deer's home is gone, when the yellow wheat that engulfed it is forgotten, when only the ants survive, emerging from their underground tunnels to have their day.

Scattered Wheat

Thanksgiving 1954. Inside the house, swishing hosiery, taffeta, laughter. My cousins and I raid the black olives and watermelon pickles off the relish tray and dash outside. The sky is fragile blue over bright corn and wheat stubble, the sun southerly, wan. We link arms and trundle over the ruts left in the farmyard by trucks and implements, four girls dressed too nicely for comfort and wearing shoes our mothers don't want us to spoil.

"Did you know you are rich?" Dian asks.

"Am not," I contend, but secretly hope the accusation is true. Dian is a foot taller than all of us and, like Judy, two years older than Vicki and me. She has a way of knowing things.

"We all are," puts in Judy. "Vicki-Dian, Judy-Julene," she chants, tap dancing like Shirley Temple on the rounded concrete roof of the storm shelter. She encourages Dian, Vicki, and me as we mimic her steps.

Across the farmyard, clods from the dirt pile thwack against the corrugated tin door of the barn. My brothers and boy cousins are having a throwing contest, while we girls take turns dropping rocks down the storm shelter vent pipe. "Hello!" Judy shouts down it, enjoying, as she always will, the sound of her own voice returning. I cup the pipe and put my mouth down over my hand. "Anybody down the-r-r-e?" I call, then make the mistake of breathing in the odor rising from the depths. Gagging, I go over to the edge of the concrete, grate my tongue off with my teeth and spit in the dry sunflower stalks.

"Hey!" my mother calls from the east porch steps. "Hey, Kids!" It's a good-humored shout, full of the same cheer I'm feeling, our everyday lives having brightened with this morning's arrival of cars.

"Maybe it's dinner," Dian says.

We trot back to the yard. The mud porch harbors cold from the night before and the smells of sheep manure on my father and brothers' coveralls, but the glass-paned kitchen door opens on action and warmth. Mom, the aunts, and Grandma hurry about with bowls and platters in their hands, gathering serving spoons, pouring gravy.

"There you are, you scamps," says Aunt Cookie, Vicki's mom. "Get yer hanies washed. Time to eat." The boys burst in the door. Cookie holds up a hand, palm outturned. "Boys, porch sink. Girls, kitchen."

Four pairs of hands under the kitchen faucet—the soap being dropped down the line. "Hey!" Judy says to Vicki, when the bar falls in the sink. "Give it to me."

"Okay," Vicki says. She picks up the soap and jams it at Judy. "Here, Shorty." Judy, who hates references to her height, grabs Vicki's hand and tries to rub her face with the soap, but Vicki twists free and starts giving Judy a wet Indian wrist burn. Dian and I back out of the way. We are used to Vicki and Judy squabbling.

"Girls, girls, girls," Mom says, stepping between them. She's wearing one of her latest creations, a red and black wool dress with gold-trimmed buttons. She made it for the state Make It Yourself With Wool contest, an event put on annually by the women's auxiliary of the Wool Growers Association. This year she's president of the auxiliary. She hands Vicki a towel. "Now go in there and tell everybody to come and get it."

The brilliant fall casts itself through the big dining room windows, but the farmstead and fields are strangely vacant of men today. They are in here, dressed in good trousers, and their ease and humor diffuse the emotion of Vicki and Judy's quarrel. My father and uncles begin moving toward the table, which, with all three leaves in it, must be ten feet long. "Don't be shy,"

Dad says to the uncle most noted for his girth.

"I won't, Harold. I think I'll just back the truck up here." He pulls out the chair nearest the kitchen supply line. We kids find places at the card tables, shoved together and covered in an olive-green cloth that matches the one on the Formica and chrome dining table. We sit with my brothers, Vicki's younger siblings, and other Bair cousins, some bigger and some littler than us. Serving dishes fly in all directions.

There is no mealtime prayer. On Sundays, Mom takes me and my brothers with her to the Emmanuel Lutheran Church in Goodland, but Dad doesn't believe in God. His own parents' faith is moderate, all their zeal going into their work.

They are here today, blessing us with a presence that we cousins, along with our parents, take for granted. We are accustomed to Grandpa's plentiful black hair streaked in silver, his hoary eyebrows, his fawn-brown eyes, and to Grandma's halo of white hair, her kind, pink face. They are Ferd and Maud, their names as common as the dirt from which most of the Bairs make their living. This time of year, the dirt is neat, ridged, and bare in the fields, except for the green stitches of winter wheat growing down the centers of the rows. The dirt, Grandpa Ferd, and Grandma Maud are among our givens. The complete list: Wheat. Distances. Faultless skies. A flat, perfectly circular horizon. Yard animals and livestock. And then there are all the intricate relations between us, some spoken, some not.

After the meal, we girl cousins retreat to my upstairs bedroom, where we take turns carding the sheepskin rug until the wool is no longer matted, but smooth like the fur on Rex, my family's border collie. Vicki and Dian lie down on the rug and begin dropping pennies through the vent grate onto Uncle Raymond's chair. We always seem to be dropping things downward, plumbing the depths. In the farmyard earlier, our little missives just struck the bottom of the cave, the sound echoing upward through the rusty pipe. This time, Dian and Vicki rear back from the grate and suppress laughter. "Kkk-mph!"

Sitting on my bed, I lean over and peer through the grate. The heel of Uncle Raymond's shiny black shoe is resting on his knee. He's holding one of the pennies between his left thumb and forefinger, turning it back and forth as if it contained a cryptic message, while smoke curls up from the cigarette he holds in his right hand. I take a deep breath, savoring not just the holiday after-dinner smells of tobacco and coffee, but also the company of girls.

"Let me see," Judy demands. Dian and Vicki move to let her crouch over the grate. She's wearing a red velvet dress and sticks her white, tights-clad rump up in the air. She stares for the longest time.

"Here, drop one," Dian whispers, shoving another penny into Judy's hand.

"No," Vicki says, having read something menacing in the way her father, my uncle Raymond, is studying the penny. "Don't!"

But Judy kisses the coin and holds it right over the center of the grate.

I hide behind my hands.

"Ouch!" Raymond shouts. The metal vent vibrates as chairs shuffle below.

Vicki, who is the most mischievous among us, would normally take command now, leading the retreat, but this time she just lets Judy squat there, focus for all the blame.

"No more of that," Dad calls up at us, his voice gruff enough to skin a cat.

I tug at the untied tails of Judy's bow as if they were reins and she a horse, but she won't budge. She remains in the same posture as before, her butt up in the air as she waits, her nose pressed against the grate. I venture a peek. Uncle Raymond is standing beside the vinyl easy chair, rubbing the bald area on top of his head. He's looking directly up at Judy. My dad would say gears are turning. Except what comes out of Raymond's mouth bears no relation to thought. "Little shit," he mumbles, and he walks out of the frame.

Judy comes backward as if she were the lightest of my dolls, the one filled with nothing but cotton fluff. Her velvet dress brushes down my front as she wilts onto the sheepskin. She lies at my feet, her face in the lanolin-smelling rug.

"Come on, Judy, get up." I tug on her bow tails, and she rises, tears trailing down her wide cheekbones.

"I told you not to," Vicki says. Vicki has pronounced cheekbones too, as does her father, Uncle Raymond. But Judy has no parents. Because of this, she gets to live with Grandma and Grandpa Bair, a fact we all envy. For one thing, she has her own swing set. Taped to my round dresser mirror is a picture of me riding the seesaw with her. I have my back to the camera, blond ponytail flying. She's beaming, in her red tam with the white fur ball on it and the red coat with the white fur trim. Behind her rises Grandma and Grandpa's large, yellow stucco house, which is five miles west of my family's farm. Their house is the biggest in this corner of Sherman County.

Sometimes after a family get-together, my cousins and I were allowed to spend the night together. We would snuggle into the hostess's bed, our legs and arms overlapping. The hostess got to sleep in the middle. I gloried in such friendly contact, for once we parted, I would return to the company of my brother Bruce. He made me hyper-conscious of my every girlish trait, mimicking my voice whenever I got excited. "Dad!" I might exclaim, running up to my father as he came in from the mud porch, his hairy forearms dripping water and smelling of Lava soap, "I jumped a bale of hay with my horse today!"

"Day-ad," would come an echo from the corner of the room, where Bruce sat reading his way through the latest stack of books he brought home from the Carnegie library in Goodland, "I jumped a bay-al of hay-ay with my horse today-ay."

When my cousins and I got together, I was suddenly elevated to an equal. They envied me, even. Dian because I lived on the farm. All of them because of my lambskin rug, my pretty pink chenille spread, my horses, and how fast I could run. Eventually, each envied me my father.

That Thanksgiving in 1954, Vicki and I were five, and Dian and Judy were seven. I had the same parents I always would. Thankfully, they have stayed alive and stayed together through all the annual celebrations, right up to today, forty-two years later. Dian had her father Carrol and my dad's sister Bernice, a movie-handsome couple whose town sophistication enthralled me. Vicki had Cookie and Raymond, who, although he lacked the sunny disposition of the other Bairs, was still hers, all hers. Judy had Grandma Maud and Grandpa Ferd.

Then came our grandparents' funerals, within two years of each other. I didn't understand then and wouldn't for years to come that their deaths portended a greater demise. I remember both their caskets, their bodies lying in strange peace—Maud's glowing white hair and the lavender wool dress she wore to all the family gatherings. I knew it still had the crisp taffeta lining, but she lay completely still and made no movement causing it to rustle.

Ferd's funeral took place in a church I'd never been to before, in Saint Francis. We arrived an hour early for the viewing. I watched him lying there, his grizzled eyebrows and his knobbed hands surrounded by the incongruous luster of white satin. I couldn't sit still, so my parents sent me outside to play. There was a concrete porch high off the ground, a good platform for daring jumps into the surrounding gravel. After a while, I heard wailing from inside, and my father came out of the building in his good brown suit, carrying Judy on his shoulder. I felt a mixture of warmth and jealousy, seeing them welded like that. It seemed right that my father would care for Judy just then. But it hurt to see my favorite perch occupied.

"Judy!" I called and ran to greet her. My father turned to walk
down the stairs, and I saw that her face was red and wet with
tears and mucous, her eyebrows wrinkled at odd angles, and
her eyes wild like a cornered badger's. She chewed on the back
of her fist as if she were a baby.

"Such a show!" came a disgusted voice from the lot. The
adults who had disliked the way Grandpa doted on Judy, spoiling her, as they believed, didn't pause to think she now had
great reason to cry.

She went to live in Alaska, with an aunt and uncle who were
seldom seen on the home front. Then she came back a few years
later to live with one of my father's younger brothers and his
wife, on a farm not far from the grandparents' old place. My
parents said she was being passed around like a piece of furniture, but I still envied her. This aunt and uncle were young
enough to be our older siblings. The uncle had a full head of
dark brown hair, whereas my dad had gone bald as the result of
a fever he got from wrestling mat burns, in high school. This
uncle didn't have the Bair paunch either, but was thin. He had
Maud's eyes, the kindest blue you could imagine. The aunt had
pert, brown hair, a huge bosom, and a bright way of speaking.
She reminded me of Annette Funicello, a new acquaintance I'd
made over our family's recently acquired TV.

Judy was now the cousin I got to see most often. Every time
her new family came over or we went there, she and I would
beg, *Can I, can she, please stay over, pl-lease?* Usually they agreed.

Studying the ground for snakes, Judy and I part
the wheat with the backs of our hands. Last summer's spilled
kernels have sprouted, and now the volunteer is thick and tall,
making it difficult to reach the grain bin doorway. Though still
green, the stalks have headed out. The bristles tickle the backs
of our thighs as we crawl inside. We marvel over the change
from outdoors to indoors—hot to cool, bright to dim. But it is
the resonance that gives the interior of the grain bin its

mystery. Outside, we were dull, ordinary farm girls, dwarfed by wind and heat and vastness. In here, the circular tin wall magnifies our voices. A few weeks from now, about July 4th, truckloads of wheat will be augered in, and the outsides of the corrugated bins will thump dully when we pat them with our hands. But right now, swept and ready, the concrete floor flaw- less, the empty bin harbors not just potential for the coming crop, but for us.

We always come here to sing. Judy's voice, even at age twelve, sounds like those we hear over my mother's almond plastic radio, which sits atop the refrigerator in our big kitchen. Her voice has twang and range. I lack her ear, but in the bin, I can hear myself and make adjustments. The echo is forgiving.

"Okay, Julene, give it your best," Judy says, and she counts, her left hand registering the beat, thumb first, then her fingers, "One, two, three, four..."

We belt out the songs we've heard over the radio. "Mona Lisa": *There could never be a portrait of my love.* Choice refrains from *The King and I* sound track: *Hello, young lovers, whoever you are, I hope your troubles are few,* and *Getting to know you, getting to know all about you.* After the duets, I sit on my haunches, lean against the wall, and listen rapt as Judy sings "Over the Rainbow." It doesn't require a great imaginative leap to picture her center stage. She stands in the beams of sun angling through the vents in the bin's dome, using her hands as confidently as Judy Garland. The fami- ly makes that comparison often. Like Garland, our Judy isn't beautiful by any ordinary standard; her face is broad in the cen- ter, as if distorted by a fisheye lens. But she has presence, show- manship. She holds her hands shoulder high, angled upward, her fingers outstretched and cradling the light that illumines her. If *happy little bluebirds fly beyond the rainbow, why oh why can't I?*

I feel as if we could fly. Kansas is the home of Dorothy not because of its drabness, but its promise. We thrive here in the vast heart of America, and the sense of connection inhabits us completely. In one of my mother's *Capper's Weeklies* I learned that the latest teen movie star, Sandra Dee, was discovered in a small town drugstore. *That could be me,* I thought. Because of the plenty our family has never had the imagination to be thankful for, the plenty that we take for granted, success and the conferral of dreams seem natural to us, passed down with our proprietorship over land. Since his death, Grandpa Ferd's eighty quarters of good wheat ground have been divvied up among all the Bair aunts and uncles, and we've known since we were children that we will also inherit. We are provided for.

When the grain bin grows too hot, Judy and I wander out to the wheat field beyond the windbreak of elms. I have always played in this field with my cousins. When we were little, we were able to lose ourselves in the wheat, but Judy and I are now tall enough that the tips of the feathery bristles brush our palms as we run, chasing a killdeer. The bird cries its name plaintively, swooping low and favoring a wing, as if injured. We know we can't catch it, but killdeers are notorious for letting you get just close enough to think you have a chance. In this way, they lead predators away from their nests. Exhausted, Judy and I crush the wheat down to make our lair. We lie on our backs, baking with the wheat, which smells a little like oven-fresh bread. We strip kernels from the heads, chewing them one at a time, careful not to swallow the bristles. They are serrated like grasshoppers' legs and will stick in your throat.

Here in the wheat we talk in ways that my brother would be sure to ridicule. Here I'm able to be a girl without shame. Today Judy begins. "Isn't it amazing how all of God's creatures have that instinct, like the killdeer?" She pauses a moment. "Mothers do anyway, that instinct to protect."

The stalks around us are turning from green to gold, each perfectly spaced and straight. Crouched low, I peer into the adjoining sun-dappled rows. "I never want to be a mother," I say.

"You don't? Why?"

I try to imagine Sandra Dee with children. But that isn't the real problem. "I'm going to be a writer. I won't have time for children."

"You can write my story. I've had quite a life already, you know."

"Mmm-mm," I say. I know Judy's life has been hard, and I empathize, but I won't have my own future commandeered in service to hers.

The edge of a cumulus cloud nudges the sun, the cooling shadow welcome on our skin. "That's Grandpa," Judy says. "Watching over us." She reaches out and pushes the skin on my thigh. The fingerprint turns white, then fills with red. "You were burning."

I've been propping myself up on my elbow, but now drop down to lie on my inner arm. I run my lips along it, enjoying the softness of this tender spot on my body, then stretch out on my side.

"I've felt him near ever since he died," Judy says. "Grandma too. But you know who I feel more than anyone?"

I take off my shoes and lie down again, thinking I could nap now in the coolness. More clouds are roiling in the south. I hear muted thunder. "Maybe Grandpa will rain. Maybe Grandma will send wind, and we'll have to run to the house, like that time when we saw the tornado."

"Oh, you!" Judy reaches down and tickles my feet. "They wouldn't do that. They would rain gentle."

"Who do you feel more than anyone?" Having gotten my jab in, I can stand another portion of Judy's self-regard.

Judy lies back, draws her legs up, and folds one foot over her knee. She stares at the cloud. "My mother. Viola. Isn't that the most beautiful name in the world? *Vi-ol-a.*"

"Where is she?"

"No one knows. I've never even met her. You know why, I think?"

"Why?"

"The court judge who took me away from her ran her off.

I know she wants me, she just doesn't have any way of getting back here for me. When I'm eighteen, I'm going to find her."

I roll over, put my chin in my hands, and stare into Judy's brown eyes. They are the color of Grandpa Ferd's and our uncles' and aunts'. Whenever I ask my parents about Judy's mother, they say that she ran away from the country with another man. It's always seemed like the deepest betrayal—leaving not only Judy, but the country and everything in it. It never occurred to me that someone might have made her leave.

"Who's your dad?" I ask, though the answer is taboo.

"You mean you don't know?"

"No." I mean yes. I mean... "Raymond?"

Tears well over the brims of Judy's eyes. She laughs. Nods. "Raymond is my dad." She falls on top of me, hugs me. Moved, I hug her back. We sit up, dust ourselves off.

"Vicki's your sister." It feels good to say this out loud. I remember one time when we all four piled onto my horse, Queenie. Dad said, "Four cousins, like bumps on a caterpillar," and I felt something wrong. One of the connections went deeper; yet between those two who were more than cousins existed a kind of minus love. I wouldn't have called it "hate" exactly.

"Half-sister," Judy corrects me.

At the noon table that day, Bruce asked, "What'd you do this morning?" He was working with Dad by then, and my brother Clark was going to college in the other end of the state. The subject that had been hardest for my father at college Ag School, organic chemistry, was easy for Clark. My oldest brother was going to be a scientist, but his absence made Bruce's lot that much more difficult to bear. He had been making tractor rounds in summer fallow west of the windbreak all morning. "I saw you in the wheat field. You looked like a couple spastics, chasing butterflies."

"We were chasing a killdeer."

"Yeah?"

"Yeah."

"That's stupid. Don't you know you can't catch a bird?"

"Someday we might. And Judy sang 'Over the Rainbow' in the grain bin. Mom, you should have heard her. It was beautiful."

"I'm sure it was, Julene." Judy's talent was a fact, but my mother avoided feeding her ego. "Now fill your plates."

Dian was the most even-tempered among us, kinder than Vicki and more realistic than Judy. She took drawing lessons from Goodland's one self-proclaimed adult artist. She drew for pleasure and didn't dream of fame the way Judy did. The family didn't make any movie star comparisons for Dian, but her muted-trumpet voice reminded me of Carol Channing. She had the wide mouth and the good teeth to complete the resemblance, although her hair was dark brown, nearly black, like her mother Bernice's. Her eyes were emerald, like those of her father, Carrol Ray. He was a debonair town man who wore gray wool trousers when he wasn't in his postman's uniform, and a straight, narrow, navy-blue tie. He had the fashionable audacity to wear pink shirts. I remember him best in a red and black plaid hunting jacket that I imagined Bernice giving him on one of their TV Christmases—the *Father Knows Best* Christmases, with him smoking a pipe, his legs folded, as Bernice, her skin smooth and amber, her lips dark red, opened foil-wrapped boxes.

They were not really as rich as they appeared. They lived their town life in a prim ranch-style just off Main Street. And they seemed plagued by bad luck—at least as far as their animals went. They'd gone through two Pekinese, a poodle, a dachshund, many kittens, and several dime store turtles and goldfish. Some got run over, others they stumbled over, some crawled off and hid until they stank. Still others died of rare-sounding diseases, such as cat leukemia, parvovirus, or epilepsy.

On our farm, we had every kind of wild pet and farm animal imaginable at some time or another, along with a thousand

ewes, who each January gave birth to twelve hundred lambs.
Dian made fascinated, fondling rounds, stroking everything that
would let her touch it. She and I stood in the wheat field out
beyond the windbreak evenings, watching the sky blaze until
night fell. The wheat glowed white in the dark. Breezes caused
it to bend and whisper around us, and, shivering, I would try
to get her to go back to the house with me. But she stood on,
watching the stars appear, naming them after her dead animals.

It's unclear to me now whether latter-day knowledge of
forthcoming tragedy casts this impression back on her, or
whether she always seemed philosophically tempered, an emis-
sary, with her green eyes, her pale skin, her height, and her dark
hair, of mortality. There came a night when death had its fill of
animals and came instead for her dad.

Some weeks later, we lay three-across beneath my pink chenille spread. Dian, Judy, and I, but not Vicki. Newly wealthy
from the sale of their land, Raymond had taken her and her
family to live in Florida. Dian said, "The night Dad died, he
came to my room."

"You mean he left the hospital and drove to your house?" I
asked.

"No, silly." Dian laughed. "He didn't leave the hospital. He
died there, of non-Hodgkin's lymphoma." She paused as the
mysterious words settled on our ears. "His spirit came to me.
He sat on my hamper. You know, my blue hamper?" Dian's
muted voice suited the spell she wished to cast, and Judy and I
listened, holding our breath. "I'd been sleeping, I think, and just
felt him there. I opened my eyes, and he was sitting with his
hands on his knees, leaning forward, looking at me. He seemed
real, except he would have been too heavy for my hamper. He'd
never sat there before. I looked at my clock, and it said twelve-
o-one—*twelve-o-one*. That's four minutes after eleven fifty-seven,
the minute Dad died."

It was Judy who broke the silence. "Why four minutes, do
you think?"

"Maybe it takes that long for the soul to leave the body," I offered.

"Or maybe he had other people to visit, like Grandma Ray." Dian paused, then said slowly, "Or maybe he'd been there for awhile."

"What did he say?" Judy asked.

"He didn't say anything. I wanted to go over and hug him, but I couldn't get up. I couldn't move. I thought he had come home, that he was well."

"What happened then?"

"I don't know. I fell back to sleep I guess. In the morning, Mom told me he was dead. And I said that was impossible. I still think it's impossible."

Judy and I both nodded. The death of someone as young as Carrol was incomprehensible. If I'd been the me of today I would have said so, and I would have braved the other thought—that it was as if people that beautiful were heaven-sent, too perfect to live here long. But I had yet to learn the art of nurture.

"What I think I felt," Dian added, "what I think woke me up was his love."

Bernice made over her garage into a beauty shop with classy black hair dryers and black sinks that seemed reminiscent of Carrol. His sophistication also lived on in Dian's voice, his good looks in her eyes. Dian had always been Carrol's daughter, but Bernice's center drifted onto Dian's little brother, who was born two months after Carrol died. Within a couple years she moved her family to a Colorado city two hundred miles from Goodland—Fort Collins, where my father had gone to college, and where a widow would have a chance at a social life.

The other member of our foursome was Vicki, Raymond's acknowledged daughter. She and her family moved into Grandpa's house shortly after his funeral. My brother Bruce and I stayed with this branch of the Bairs for a few days that

summer, when my mother was recovering from an illness.
Cookie wanted us to take afternoon naps, but Bruce and Vicki
were a natural pair, attuned in orneriness. They would slip out
the bedroom window, and I would follow, scurrying to play out
in the machine sheds, where we wouldn't be noticed.

One afternoon, Vicki and Bruce, going hand over hand and
toe over toe like monkeys, scaled the ree-bar rafters of the
largest quonset. They dangled up there like monkeys, giggling
over a secret I was dying to be let in on. Finally Vicki called to
me, "Come here!"

"Where?"

"Here!" She pointed to a spot directly beneath her. I looked
up expectantly. She dropped a pigeon egg on my forehead. By
the time I stopped crying, I noticed that she and Bruce were
gone, vanished into thin air, as my mom liked to say. And they'd
taken my sandals. Vicki had summer-toughened feet, but I
couldn't negotiate the sticker patch. I stood in front of the shed,
wailing, until Cookie, roused from her own much-needed nap,
came and rescued me.

Cookie's hair was dried auburn, as if bleached that way
from too many perms. It reminded me of the scraggly, windblown elms and the dusty heat, the unfenced yard outside. The
house had decayed inside since the departures, in death, of the
grandparents. It seemed hollowed out, the furniture sparse and
drab. But Cookie was pretty, her voice melodious, pianissimo,
assuring. You never heard her yelling at her kids.

"Don't let that Vicki and Bruce get yer goat. They're both
just full of the devil," she said admiringly. She gave me a cool
washcloth to wipe my tears. "You like cinnamon sugar or oat-
meal cookies best? Cinnamon sugar? I thought so." She poured
me a glass of milk. Each morning and evening she milked the
Guernsey to fill bottles for Vicki's baby brother. Raymond never
lifted a finger, but Cookie didn't complain. Beyond the kitchen,
I could see him pacing up and down the hallway on the green
wool runner, smoking a cigarette, his eyes wild beneath his

receding hair, which was gray already, even though he was only in his thirties.

Today Dad tells me no one knows for sure what went wrong with Raymond. "He could never do anything right, as far as Ferd was concerned," Dad says. And it alarms me to think that my gentle grandfather, who often gave me quarters to sit in his lap, would have displayed anything but kindness toward his youngest son. "Then Mom," Dad says, "would always bail him out when he got in trouble." He is being literal. Raymond was arrested several times for public drunkenness and fighting. Vicki believes her father might have been hyperactive in childhood, an affliction she also suffered and which no one understood then. Raymond's hyperactivity, if that's what his problem was, played itself out in adulthood through hyper-mobility. He moved Cookie and his family sixteen times during their fifteen-year marriage, at one point winding up back at the grandparents' house for a second time.

Dad said Raymond had pissed away his inheritance. Part of that pissing must have gone to buy Vicki the little powder-blue motor scooter I so greatly envied. From my point of view, it seemed anyone who lived at the grandparents' place got all the perks, as if Grandpa enchanted them, even from beyond the grave. First it had been Judy and her pretty red clothes, the swing set, the Easy Bake oven, and a roomful of dolls, and now, Vicki, the scampiest scamp among us, had the blue scooter. It wasn't just blue, but powder blue, its fenders voluptuously rounded like a Corvette's. It was the most daring, seductive plaything I'd ever encountered, and Vicki was generous with it, letting me ride it by myself down to the mailbox, a mile from the house.

She had let go of her childish roguery and had graduated to a new kind of mischief. I remember Dian and I sitting in her bedroom, which long ago had been Judy's, poring over a Frederick's of Hollywood catalogue with her. We each dreamed of wearing the sexy negligees, our breasts pointed, our backs arched, our long hair swaying above our hips, but only Vicki placed any orders. She adorned her snappy brown eyes in false lashes, combed her sable hair down over one eye as did Veronica Lake, and wore the lace bras beneath thin white blouses to school.

The last time I remember all of us together was for another family dinner at our farm. Vicki and I were thirteen, Dian and Judy fifteen. Previous years at bedtime, intrigued by the waves of laughter coming from downstairs, we put our ears to the vent grate to hear the dirty jokes the adults were telling, but now our own conversation fascinated us more than theirs. Dian told us her theory about how "it" was done.

"The guy," she explained, "puts a pillow under you so you'll be high enough up for him to get in."

I kept my hands folded over my stomach and had opted for the far side instead of the middle of the bed. "Does it hurt?" I asked.

She laughed her Carol Channing laugh, benevolent, adult. "Maybe the first time." I could almost see her wide smile in the darkness. "But I bet it hurts good."

"I'm going to wait," Judy declared.

"Me too," I said.

"When you meet someone you love, you'll want to, Julie," Vicki advised.

"I have something more important to do first." That declaration from Judy.

We all waited silently for the ritual telling of Judy's story, culminating in Judy's obsession. When she turned eighteen, she would run away and find her mother. It was the boldest dream any of us harbored. A departure from the lives laid out for all of us, as wives, it was a rebellious rejection of the male protection that had proven less than satisfactory in Judy's case. Not only was Raymond, who didn't acknowledge her anyway, broke, but the dashing young uncle Judy now lived with was on the verge of bankruptcy. Grandpa Ferd had told Judy he would leave her a share of his property, but he'd never gotten around to writing her into the will. And no one had championed her, no one had defended her against the siblings' greed.

"When I find her," Judy said, "I'm going to prove them all wrong."

"About what?" Vicki asked, even though we all knew.

"She is not a whore."

The harsh label hung in the air, ready to drop onto any one of us. If we had sex with boys and the word got out, we too would be called whores. Whereas the boys, our own family example had taught us, would be held blameless. Finally Vicki said, "No. Of course she isn't." Raymond and Cookie had divorced by then, and it touched me to note that Cookie's warmth had crept into Vicki's voice—even when talking to Judy.

My sense of kinship with Dian and Vicki evaporated as boyfriends came into their lives, then babies. Later that year, Vicki got "knocked up," in the local terminology, and married a boy known as a hood. Dian got pregnant by her Fort Collins boyfriend. She married him, but soon got divorced, and Bernice moved the family back to Goodland, which she thought would be a better place to raise her grandson, a new male on whom to center herself. The aunt and uncle Judy lived with lost their farm and moved to Boulder, where the uncle now sold real estate. I visited her in the summer when I was fifteen. We spent most of our time trekking around the city in pursuit of a boy Judy liked. And then I had my first tremendous kiss in her basement from a football player relative of our aunt's. Our quest for romance had overshadowed our interest in each other. Shortly after that visit, Judy vanished.

It was my young aunt, Judy's adopted mother, who called, divulging the news to my mother. We lived in town by then, in the house my parents had finally felt secure enough in their wealth to build, and I remember pondering the news in my new bedroom that smelled of knotty pine, fresh paint, and the wool carpet, which was royal blue. Judy had never seen the room, and I had often imagined how she would react when she did. Her prominent cheeks would shine like lightbulbs, and she would say, "Oh Julie, Julie, Julene." But now she had disappeared as if into a void. The police were called, but had no clues. Did I know anything? I told about the boyfriend, but his had been the first place they checked. He still lived with his father in an uncompleted house in the foothills overlooking what he had poetically referred to as a "lap full of stars," the lights of Boulder.

Judy would have been better off if she'd run away with him. Weeks later, my aunt received a letter from Judy. She had ridden her bike to the Crossroads Mall and met Viola's husband there. Ed. I hesitate to call him Judy's stepfather, since Judy had never lived with Viola. Judy had secretly planned the meeting for months. Ed escorted her back to Fresno, California, to her mother.

It was as if Ed had reached down in the wheat field after a spring rain and pulled up an entire plant. That Judy had gone with him seemed proof of all the hurt she'd felt, which for years had been dismissed as overacting, as the melodramatic imaginings of a spoiled child. Despite her breathtaking boldness, I didn't feel she was better off in the new circumstances. I thought of Black Beauty, our favorite story character when we were little, of how that promising horse had been swiped from the pasture of its youth.

A year or so later, even more shocking news arrived. Judy and Ed, who was at least twenty years Judy's senior, had run away together, abandoning Judy's long-sought mother, Viola. Judy never explained how this tryst evolved. She didn't write to me. Some years later, regretting my own mistakes with men, I believe that, like all of us, Judy craved male love. Now I understand that Judy may not have made the choice willingly. Ed *was* much older. Judy *was* displaced and vulnerable. Judy accepted the consequences in isolation and silence, as if she were to blame.

My father's substantial love and reliability should have given me the confidence to put off boyfriends' advances. It should have centered me in my own worth, but his stardom in our family only convinced me I needed a man to call my own, someone to validate me. I had my first sex at sixteen, the year following Judy's disappearance, in the backseat of a blue, 1959 Chevy Impala, with a boy named Mick from a tiny nearby town. He didn't excite me in the least, although I pretended he did. There was something in his stupid behavior—the telling of bad, usually dirty jokes, the popping of bubble gum, the perennial combing of greasy hair, the self-conscious smoking of Marlboros, the drinking of beer, and the burning of tire rubber on pavement—that told me if I didn't put out he wouldn't call anymore. And I wanted to have dates.

Decades of missteps followed on Mick—compromising relationships and two marriages in which I betrayed myself in favor of that longed-for continuation of male approval. I lived, as I had between my childhood visits with my cousins, surrounded almost entirely by males. Most of my friends were men, and I felt this distinguished me, set me apart from other women. I seldom thought of Judy, Dian, and Vicki, but when I did, I felt superior to them. I married a boy from a wealthy midwestern manufacturing family and left for San Francisco. We took part in the glamorous times, running a recording studio and selling audio equipment to rock bands. Then, after my second, short-lived marriage to an abusive drunk, I landed back at my parents' house in Kansas, the one they had built in town when I was sixteen. I hadn't been better or smarter than my cousins, just luckier. Pregnant and broke at age thirty-five instead of age fifteen, I now felt dumber.

I was in this frame of mind the afternoon we received a call from the nearly grown child of one of my cousins.

Mom was out somewhere and Dad was at the farm. Wanting to earn my keep and wanting to prove myself capable of doing men's work, I'd been driving a tractor that morning, sowing wheat. I had come back into town to get a replacement for a broken drill tube. I was at that stage of my pregnancy when I had to pee all the time, so I had stopped by the house to use the bathroom.

I picked up the aqua princess phone, which matched the aqua sink and stove in my mother's kitchen, and heard a voice that sounded distantly familiar. When I discovered who it was, I dropped the hurry I was in, pulled out the chair Mom kept in the telephone nook, and sat down, stretching my legs out and resting my hand on my belly. I had been pretending I wasn't tired, and secretly welcomed the excuse to rest and talk awhile.

We exchanged niceties about the past. And in truth, my relationships with my cousins seem interchangeable, given the upshot—our all having come to the same eventual pass. "Mom says she was kinda mean to you when you were little." That would be Vicky. "...that she always loved visiting your farm because of all the animals." Dian. "...that you used to sing together in the grain bins." Judy.

"Chicken again," Dad said at supper that night. A disappointment as far as he was concerned. He spooned one of the de-skinned, cornflake encrusted thighs out of the Pyrex baking dish. "Gawd, how I'd love a big T-bone steak."

"Well," Mom said, defensively. "You know what that does to your cholesterol."

"You're going to keep me alive, aren't you?" Dad joked. "You'll get several more crops out of me yet."

"It's up to you. Another dozen, if you'll stop sneaking spoonfuls of peanut butter and slices of cheese." Mom had put Dad on a diet after the first diagnosis of heart disease. He had since lost twenty pounds, along with a good percentage of the cholesterol in his blood.

I dished up conservative helpings of beans and chicken, cut open my baked potato, mashed in a teaspoon of margarine—

less than I would have used were I not party to Mom's campaign
to keep my father with us.

"John got that part back on the drill okay for you, didn't
he?" Dad asked me. Both my brothers had long since turned
down the farm and gone on to other careers. Clark taught
chemistry in a junior college in California. Bruce wrote for the
newspaper in Hays, a town over a hundred miles east of
Goodland, where his wife taught at the college. My return gave
Dad hope that one of his children would take over the farm.

"Yeah. I got in another five rounds."

"Go-ood!" Dad put a humorous twist on the word, lowering his voice so that the "ood" was solid and smooth, a level
floor.

I told them about the phone call from my cousin's child.
The upshot—my cousin, my parents' niece, needed money to
leave an abusive man.

Mom set her iced tea down. "Oh, that bastard!"

Dad went on eating. "I always knew he was good for noth-
in'."

I leaned forward, sure they saw it my way. "So we need to
help her."

"Well, I don't know..." my mother said, and I felt myself
tensing.

"You don't want to get mixed up with domestic squabbles,"
Dad added.

Mom shoved her tea glass along the gold lines embossed in
the oval table top. "If she needed money, then she should have
called herself."

I smoothed the clean frock I'd changed into from the overalls and work shirt I'd worn drilling wheat. Following in my
mother's steps, I had made the frock myself, not with wool, but
with cotton, on her Singer. I tried to calm myself. If I became
strident, they would balk.

Dad grabbed another piece of chicken. "It never pays to go
messing in other people's affairs."

Mom dragged the glass back toward her plate, trailing a napkin behind it. "If we sent the money, that jerk would just get his hands on it."

She looked at me, and I thought I detected uncertainty, or openness at least to my point of view. "If I'd stayed with Dwayne, you don't know what might have happened. But you helped me get out. And I thank you for it."

"That's different," Dad said.

"Yes, it is." This from Mom.

I shoved my plate forward, my food half-eaten. "How is my situation any different? I wasn't a whole lot smarter than her, it turned out."

"You said it." Dad's chair rumbled over the linoleum as he pushed back from the table. "But," he said over his shoulder as he left the room, "you've been showing some brains lately."

Mom laughed, relieved the issue was decided. "And don't forget. You're our daughter."

Dad padded across the living room rug in the clean white socks he put on after his shower, which he'd taken every night for as long as I could remember. In from the field, shower, shave, supper. He lifted his glasses from the mantel and the *Goodland Daily* from the table beside his chair, his throne. He settled in, sending the recliner's leg rest out with a finality I'd learned long ago to heed. Conversation ended. Subject closed.

I lay in the blue bedroom, the one they had commissioned for me when I was sweet sixteen and screwing Mick in the back of his Impala. I'd been out and around since then, a big loop that took in a lot of the world. Only to wind up back here. But with a mind now, with some awareness. I hadn't been a complete fool for my second husband. I was not as dumb as a fifteen-year-old. I married him knowing he was an alcoholic, but thinking him worth the risk. If he started drinking again, I would leave. He slapped me, sent me careening across the kitchen, then held me against the wall, his hands on my throat. I did leave him, but may not have if there had been nowhere to turn.

I remembered Judy's cheeks smeared with tears, her face red and anguished as she rode on my father's shoulder down the steps of the church in Sainty. Why wouldn't he carry this cousin now? I'd been convinced my parents would feel her pain as if it were their own, but that was only the way I felt it, so recently escaped from my own abusive husband. I hadn't gone back to college yet. The word "patriarchy" didn't leap into my mind—the narrow definition of family, the way surnames enforce the ownership of women and land. I hadn't begun to wonder how different things might be in a matriarchy. All I knew was that the humiliation I felt at my husband's rage resembled in an unsettling way how I felt that moment as my father's protected daughter.

I reached out and fingered the bumps on the blue glass lamp shade. The lamp was an imitation of the kerosene lanterns I'd seen in western movies. As a teenager I had loved the way the room combined horsy elements with luxury. I'd felt proud of my parents, all the hard work they'd done making the house possible. Their success had seemed to confer dignity on me. But I'd done nothing special to win my privileges then or now—a roof over my head, my angry husband already a memory. Dad was right. I didn't know what my cousin's true situation was. But when I had needed help, there had been no hesitation. Luck of birth granted me my good fortune. Nothing else.

I stood up, walked across the room, and leaned on the blue counter of the built-in sink. I studied my eyes in the mirror. I could see my mother's green in them more than my father's brown, yet I'd always identified with the Bairs. I was becoming a mother for the first time while my cousins' kids were all grown, or nearly so. Vicki's daughter, Trina, was making every-one proud. She'd gone through college on a basketball scholar-ship and had recently been accepted into medical school. Judy and Ed lived in Nashville, gone there to pursue a music career, not for Judy, but for their daughter Linda. On top of the stereo console in my parents' living room rested a demo record Linda had made. Dad played it often, tapping his foot along to the gospel music and asking me with a note of familial pride if I didn't think Linda was as good as Tammy Wynette. But Dian and Vicki's sons had both gotten their girlfriends pregnant. Progress on some fronts, history repeating itself on others.

Standing behind my closed veneer door with its smooth sheen, I held my hand out horizontally in front of me, the fingers spread, and looked down at it. My veins were like my mother's, prominent and blue. Would my child trace the veins in my hands the same way I had hers? I would push one down, watch the blood swell up in a bubble, then let go. At the supper table, my mother's hands had betrayed the debate within her as she nervously pulled her iced tea glass back and forth. If it were up to her, would she have said yes?

"Isn't it amazing," Judy had said, "how mothers have that instinct to protect?"

I flew my hand away from my belly, swooping it low, dragging the little finger like a broken wing. "Kill-deer!" I keened.

Housewives, Fieldhusbands

I stir my box of Lincoln Logs with one of the long, half-round pieces. Finally, the Revlon-red chimney appears, wedged under the gritty flaps at the bottom of the box. The weightless balsa cutout rests like a kiss on the peak of the green roof. My cabin is built and just about ready for transport to its sacred spot at the center of the blue-glass coffee table.

Holding my breath at the noise made by the overhead, concealed rollers, I slide our living room's varnished pine door open just enough to squeeze through. I creep across the open terrain of the dining room, avoiding squeaky places in the floor. My mother is in her sewing room with the machine running, so I feel momentarily safe in the kitchen. I pull open the junk drawer in the metal sink cabinet and lift out the flashlight. I also get the spray bottle full of vinegar water, and grab one of Mom's embroidered dishtowels from the refrigerator door. Back in the living room, I push the door shut again, then close the venetian blinds. The mauve-furnished, floral-carpeted sanctuary glows dark and violet.

The mystical aura is perfect for the rites I'm about to undertake, but the wind undermines the mood. It moans through the eaves and whistles through the sashes of the windows, filtering fine dust onto the sills. Dad said this morning, "If it blows again like yesterday, we'll be cutting tomorrow—if it don't hail, that is." I know the whole country counts on this south wind to ripen the wheat, but it robs mornings of promise and makes summer afternoons a weary trial. Outside our windows, the branches of the old elms and locust trees creak and bob, on the verge of breaking. The leaves toss, revealing their gray undersides.

Dust devils churn down the gullies in the summer fallow across from the house. Thistles and devil's claws—the gray, thready, dual-pointed pods of wild gourds—roll across the farmyard. To go outside requires wearing one of the stale-smelling cotton scarves that hang from the hooks on the porch, to prevent my fine blond hair from tangling and filling with dirt. I would have to wear jeans too, in the ninety degree heat, because of blowing yard sand, which stings like needles on bare legs. Even inside, I feel as if I'm under siege—my skin and hair getting dirtier by the minute.

I squirt vinegar water onto the coffee table glass and wipe it clean, then lift the cabin, which I built over the two longest half-round logs. Imagining it being carried like the Arc of the Covenant, on the shoulders of two Israelites, I lower it gently onto the table. The cabin contains no written commandments, only tacit ones that I don't even realize I'm heeding. The glass is French blue, my mother tells me—the deep, irresistible cobalt of Evening in Paris perfume bottles. As a toddler, I used to lie across this table, spreading my arms wide. I remember in the tender skin of my belly and shoulders how cool and smooth the glass was. I used to draw my lips between my teeth and rub my mouth back and forth, then watch the fog I'd breathed onto the surface evaporate.

I hold the flashlight beneath the glass and shine it upward. With my chin on the mahogany table edge, I stare through the cabin's windows at the indwelling light. I hear Mom walk past the closed door behind me. On the verge of being discovered at worship, I press my hand over my lips and hold my breath, but her steps fade toward the kitchen. I imagine the cabin is my house and I am twenty, married to Adam, the most rakish and dangerous of Ben Cartwright's sons. Thou shalt marry. Thou shalt marry well. Twenty seems a terribly long time to wait, but that's how old my mother was when she married. Adam has built me this house in the center of a lake on the Ponderosa, in Montana, where, instead of lifting field dirt, a clean wind rushes through tall pines.

I don't wonder why I feel shame; I just do. I'll leave it to my future, adult self to note that I have closed out the real day and replaced it with manufactured light. In the living room, alone, the door pulled closed, the shade drawn, I revolve in the very womb of withdrawal. This is the softest room in the house, even though the easy chair and couch are covered in an abrasive pile weave and the carpet is scratchy wool, doesn't reach the walls, and has no pad under it. The light filters around the edges of the blinds through the white sheer curtains, which my mother tells me are made of spun fiberglass. I come in here to fantasize, to imagine my future.

Suddenly, men's voices rattle along the wide door panels and along the back of my rib cage. I flick off the flashlight and shove it under the couch, where it rolls noisily off the edge of the carpet onto the pine floor. I pick up the cabin and wreck it back into the box, which I hide behind the lounger. I open the blinds and, lacking any other exit, shove the door back into the wall, hoping the noise will mask my embarrassment.

The men are standing with their backs to the living room, looking out the big bay windows. Among them is my brother Bruce, who is fifteen. My older brother, Clark, would be here also if he hadn't opted to attend summer school at K-State. He is so smart that he graduated high school valedictorian last year, at only seventeen. Bruce, my father, and the hired men—Hank, Uncle Raymond, Earl—stand in their stocking feet, having removed their work boots in the mud porch. But they still wear all their other armor—heavy denim jeans or overalls, blue or gray work shirts, sun-blackened skin. The house grows darker as clouds edge over us. Mom switches the lights on. The wind has stopped, and, punctuated by the sound of distant thunder, rain patters on the roof. The scent of cool air, the smell of dampening dust, freshens my outlook on not just the afternoon, but life. My mother and I will run our rags over all the furniture, where the gleam of wood and glass will last at least until the fields dry out and the dust begins to blow again.

I wedge myself between my dad and Bruce to stand before the middle window. I expect Dad to place the flat of his palm on my head and press; I expect to receive the usual playful hazing, but he is so focused on the impending storm that he doesn't even notice me. Something inside me trills along with the mounting force of the wind as it returns in earnest, from the north now. Lightning snaps. We are negatives, our forms inscribed on the surface of the single bright instant. I hunch reflexively, trying to shelter from the immediate thunder. But there is no hiding from such noise. I look around and above us, half-expecting to see our house shaken to rubble, destroyed as readily as my log cabin. Beside me, Dad hasn't flinched. He's standing with his arms dangling, slightly bent at the elbow. His muscle-rounded shoulders seem to tilt even more forward than usual. His striped overalls hang off him as if he were a statue.

On the other side of Bruce stands Mom, a fresh dishtowel draped over her shoulder. I cringe a little, knowing she found the other towel gone. She embroidered this towel last winter. It has a fanciful design of two puppies frolicking, one brown, one black. They are tugging on a red rope, its ends looping prettily and tied off in frayed knots. She wears a housedress, which she also made. Her legs are bare except for white anklets and the Ace bandage she wraps daily to stop her varicose veins from hurting. Another bolt and the electricity goes out. The dark afternoon moves into the house itself, the air suddenly chill. We are all lined up here—mother and father, brother and sister, the hired men—all equally dependent on what the sky does. Only Uncle Raymond seems unaffected by the storm. Perennially tired, he left the window after the first lightning crack and sat down at the Formica dining table.

The rain isn't just falling anymore, but driving southward in a sheet. We watch the front move past the barn and into the sumac south of the house, where the stalks bend before it. Dad is untouchable now, his jaw set and angry. I notice he has forgotten to remove his battered work hat. I can't bear to be next to him, in the position I've always vied with Bruce for. I retreat and draw a chair up to the table beside Uncle Raymond, whose apathy, at the moment, appeals to me more than my father's involvement. "Hey, Unc," I say, and he pats me once, kindly, on the head and turns his gaze back to where it was before, on the sugar bowl.

Raymond is my cousin Vicki's dad. They came back from Florida a year ago, where Dad says he "just piddled," losing all the money he inherited from Grandpa Bair. Now they live in Grandpa's old place, five miles west of ours. Raymond hires on to help my father during the busiest times. He'll be driving truck this harvest, if there is a harvest.

The hail starts sporadically, a slow death of hope, one thunk! of ice against the roof, then two within the same instant, stones hurled by something that isn't God, my dad would insist. What "shits" these stones—that's his word for it—doesn't think and doesn't care. We watch the white balls pelt the trees and bounce off the sidewalk. Soon we can no longer see the barn through the whiteness. The tumult puts a brilliant end to a day of wind and dirt, thrilling me even as the leaves are being stripped from the trees and from Mom's rosebushes, even as every wheat bud, at least in the nearby fields, is being pounded into the ground.

My father and the men linger after the hail has moved on. No one owns umbrellas or raincoats. It rains seldom in our part of Kansas, and so briefly that we just wait it out. The lights don't come back on, so Mom goes into the kitchen to find the candles. Even though it's only four o'clock, the sky is still dark, and we all want something, some flame to hover around. I hear her digging through the sink drawer. "Well, criminently," she says. "Where's the flashlight?" I don't tell her where it is. She manages to find the candles without the flashlight, and she and I drip wax onto saucers.

Dad sits in his lounger at the far corner of the room. I've never seen him so removed. I look back and forth between his under-lit face and Uncle Raymond's, whose broad cheeks seem even wider than usual. The candles cast undulating shadows up around Raymond's eyes, and two tufts of kinky gray hair sprout from the edges of his shiny scalp. Despite his frozen posture, there's an odd energy about Raymond. He's mulling something—some old hurt. I've heard Dad say that Grandpa was cruel to him. "He always told him he was worthless."

I can see Dad's chest heaving; he's breathing purposefully, huffing almost, as if to exert control at least over this much of nature, himself. I can feel the slackness inside his cheeks as if I were inside him, my own jaw hanging slightly open beneath closed lips, the spit forming faster than normal, an adrenal drenching. His jaw and brown eyes have released his anger at the impersonal force of nature, and he is computing how to recover. He is figuring already, ten minutes after the storm, what it will take in manpower, in time, in machinery, in seed, to disk the wheat under and plant millet, the only crop that might mature this late if the first frost comes no earlier than the usual September twentieth. After a rain like this, it'll be four days at least before he can get back in the field. Dad is a born farmer. Grandpa had him driving teams of six horses in the fields when he was only ten. Even though he went to college and had other options, he came back to farm. He'll persevere. We all depend on this. Hank and Earl go out the dining room door to stand on the porch. Raymond gets up absently and follows them. We immediate family members carry our candles into other rooms.

           Unconsciously, on afternoons such as that one, I knew that while my mother and I might suffer deprivations due to the storm, we were lucky not to be male. A man had to keep moving, out in the void of the bigger world. The climate of western Kansas was harsh, the land huge and daunting. It fell to men to wage enterprise across that distance. A man had to keep spinning, like a gyroscope, the force of his energy keeping his family in balance. If he lost heart, if the emptiness of the Plains got inside him, slowing his movement until he shuffled over the dirt the way Uncle Raymond did rather than stomping like my father, if the heat and hugeness wearied him so that he craved the cool interior of the house, if he couldn't face a shattered crop, but sat and let weeds take the field, if he failed to spin, he and his family would topple. My father never contemplated slowing down. He never allowed any pain to distract him from the field task at hand.

Dad was always just in from outside, and power and energy accompanied each entrance, as if sunlight and wind came in with him. "Yass-min," he would call, with exaggerated lilt as he leaned in the kitchen doorway. "Oh Yass-min! Towel, Yass-min." It wasn't that his German ancestry still carried over in his speech; he just enjoyed poking fun at Mom's Swedish heritage, and he liked the slightly off-color sound of "Yass."

"Ooohhh, wait a minute, damn it!" My mother would come grumbling from a far corner of the house where she'd been immersed in a chore, perhaps ironing sheets on the big roller ironer, the mangle, as it was incongruously called. All seriousness, angry with herself, she would scurry into the washroom behind the kitchen and reemerge with a towel proffered. "Here," she would say. "Here's the damned thing. I forgot to put it out, I guess."

"Thank you, Yass-min," Dad would say, his voice humorously melodic.

After the hail, my father wouldn't be in a teasing mood for months. From my perspective, that would be the hugest cost of the storm—the loss of my father's light.

My mother wasn't entirely an indoor creature. She had many outdoor chores. She milked the cow, raised chickens and vegetables, and tended an immense, beautiful flower garden. During summers, after both brothers had been deemed old enough to begin working with the men, I would often sleep in. On waking, I would look out my east window first thing. It reassured me to see my mother in the yard, bent over her hoe,

weeding the roses or her irises. To protect her skin, she always
wore garden gloves, a bonnet, and a long, light-colored cotton
blouse over her housedress. Even though dressed protectively,
she appeared completely confident and managerial. When the
weather cooperated, she coaxed beautiful life out of the dirt, as
if her hoe were a wand and she a magician. The yard belonged
to her, she to it, just as the house and she co-owned each other.

I would go downstairs, pour myself a bowl of cereal to eat
at the dining room table, and in she would come, swinging the
dining room door open before removing her bonnet and
stomping her feet on the mud porch mat. "Lord," she would
say, invoking the entity she did believe in, but with none of the
sanctimony that my father disliked in some of our neighbors.
"It's getting hot out there." Energized by the morning and her
work, she would stride over and flip the switch on the window
air conditioner.

I would rinse my bowl, leave it in the sink, and go outside
to stretch in the warmth. I strolled past the flowers, their pur-
ples, reds, and pinks intense under the sprinklers Mom had left
going in the beds. I said good morning to all the yard animals
and ventured up past the chicken coop and granary to the shop.
Sometimes I visited when the men were working. Amidst their
cussing, they would look my way and caution each other with
glances. Often they'd be welding and would warn me to close
my eyes or turn my back so as not to be blinded. Bang, clank,
clank—hammers on steel. All shop activities involved a lot of
pounding, but usually the building only echoed the presence of
the men, who spent most of their time in the fields.

My father made no pretense of cleanliness. He left his tools
scattered over workbenches that were coated in a half-inch layer
of dust and grease. Big clumps of dried mud, having fallen from
implements, lay on the shop floor amidst pools of oil and
spilled grain. The clods had sticker and kochia weeds embedded
in them, and numerous bugs roved about, ants nibbling away
chunks from the carcasses of grasshoppers, or beetles rolling

balls of dung toward the stairs leading down into the shop basement. The basement still housed the implements my mother's father had used on this same farm—plowshares and harness trees, all blended to yellow-brown in color by a coat of dust and condensed oil. I would take a step or two down the stairs and peer in. Just enough dim light fell through the south window to highlight a complex city of spider webs, many belonging to black widows, common in our region. A jumbled mass of old boxes, chains, gears, fan belts, tubing, and scrap iron competed for both floor and wall space. Often I'd watched Dad saunter down the stairs into the cavern to retrieve a piece of iron for welding, but standing on those stairs myself, the dank air breathing up at me, I would begin to imagine salamanders and spiders crawling up my ankles. I would scamper back up the steps, stamp my feet, and swipe my hands over my clothes and through my hair.

When the day became too hot for me I would return to the house and discover that my mother had entered into her unquestioned and unquestioning routine. At ten in the morning, she might be kneading cinnamon roll dough. I sat on the kitchen counter and sprinkled the sugar on for her. If she didn't have another chore for me, I might build a fort under the dining room table, do headstands against the living room wall, or ride a pillow down the uncarpeted hall stairs. Once monthly, Mom waxed the floors of the dining room and front entry, disturbingly cutting me off from all but the kitchen and the pantry. I didn't like not having access to my house. For it *was* my house, almost more than my mother's. I owned it in the manner of a luxuriating house cat, normally free to wander the rooms and loll in any of them. When the wax dried, though, its sheen captivated me and seemed worth the sacrifice. The linoleum looked like real hardwood flooring, and Mom bragged about how it had fooled many a visitor.

My mother's and father's realms seldom intermingled. She seldom set foot in the shop her father, Grandpa Carlson, had

built. She would send me up there—"up" because the shop was
north of the house—to get a pair of pliers or her hoe, which
Dad had taken to sharpen on the grinder and then forgotten to
return. Although she loved working in the soil of her garden,
on the rare occasion when she came in contact with grease or
machinery, you could almost see her begin to wither, as did
Superman before kryptonite. I inherited my childhood dislike
of wind from her. "Confounded wind!" she would say, coming
in from an errand up at the chicken house or in her yard.
During wheat harvest, when the big combines moved through
all the surrounding fields like giant, robotic insects, Mom
would take dinner out to the very edge of the uncut wheat in
the trunk of her car.

These were the only times I saw her in the fields. She leaned
over the trunk, sprung the lid, then lifted the tablecloth off her
Corning Ware. Together we served fried chicken, green beans,
dinner rolls, and my favorite potatoes, cut in large hunks that
she first boiled, then fried in butter. The combine and truck
drivers, sitting on a blanket Mom had placed in the scant shade
of the biggest wheat truck, inhaled the scrumptious food in
shifts. The noon sun reflected off the stubble as if it were real
gold, causing us all to squint as we watched the progress of the
harvest in our own and neighbors' fields. Summer thrummed
up out of the ground. But Mom didn't enjoy the picnic much
herself. The wind lofted the smells of engine grease and fried
chicken across the wastes while she, having little appetite under
the circumstances, swatted at flies and, in response to the dust
kicked up by passing trucks, said "ew-ugh!"

Coming into the house, the men, obversely, entered civi-
lization, ease. The farmstead, with its windbreak of elms, the
house at center, formed a rare oasis in a landscape where farms
were two or more miles apart. After the big light of the outdoors, the house's interior felt refreshingly protective—cool in
the summertime, warm and emanating baking aromas in the
winter. In the summer, the men came in just before dinner and

collapsed into big easy chairs in front of the air conditioner, their knees splayed, their Red Wings resting hugely on turned feet. Their guards came down once they were inside, and they relaxed with abandon. My brothers made a show of this, throwing their arms wide, letting their hats hang from one hand. A ring circled their foreheads where the hats had rested.

I had my chores, too, most of which seemed fun. I skated the dust mop over the pine boards in the upstairs hallway, mashed the potatoes, set the table for meals, washed the dishes, dried and sorted silverware into the drawer as rapidly as machine-sorted change. I warmed milk, poured it into quart-sized Coke bottles, fastened nipples over them, and fed the "bum" or orphaned lambs. I also thought it would be fun to drive tractors.

Every summer meal, I would accost my father as he came in from the mud porch. "Can I drive the tractor this afternoon, Dad?" Day in, day out, we had the same conversation.

Not hearing, Dad takes one of the homemade dinner rolls from the platter I'm holding, sits down, butters the roll, and begins munching, no other food on his plate.

"Dad!" I say again, sitting down across from him. "Can you give me a lesson driving tractor today?"

"Julene." Mom's tone is a reprimand.

"I'll give her a lesson," Bruce says, getting up from his easy chair, coming to the table, and taking his place beside Dad. "She can drive the 4010. I'll do her job. What is her job?"

"I don't want to learn from you. I'll take my lessons from Dad."

Dad finally notices me. "You want to disk the summer fallow with me? You're going to have to stick it out, though. I can't be stopping to ..."

Mom interrupts him. "No daughter of mine is going to bake out there on a tractor like a man. And it's too dangerous, Harold. For crying out loud."

"That's right," Dad concedes.

"Lucky little shit," Bruce says.

Not noticing him, Dad says, "You can lose an arm or a leg in the blink of an eye."

I know Dad is thinking about the time his leg was caught in some machinery and he spent two months in the hospital. I remember his absence vividly, although I was only four at the time. Clark took me onto the lawn outside the hospital window and held me up to wave to him. But all I can think of now is what I can't have. I narrow my eyes and try to make Bruce wither.

"Chow down, people," Mom says. "We've got a special dessert today. Julene's trying out cookie recipes for 4-H."

My father takes a brownie and makes an exaggerated show of his approval, then turns to Bruce and addresses him like the man he is becoming, "Don't forget to refuel before you take that rig over west. And did you grease this morning?"

It would have been an honor for me to do my brother's work, but demeaning for him to lift a plate from the table or wield a broom. Everyone tacitly understood that through the men's largess, we females were allowed the luxuries of the house and yard, but these comforts entailed a compromise in status. Only on the first Friday of each summer month did I partake of our luxury with little regret. These were club days, charmed days. As my mother and I zoomed past the fields full of men on open air tractors, my resentment and envy of my brother dissolved.

We arrive at the Rickard's behind the Roder's car. Opal Seaman pulls in behind us. We all sit for a moment with the windows rolled up to let the dust settle. Then, if the scene could be witnessed from an invisible, floating blimp sent to revisit the era, the passenger and drivers' doors of our square-bumpered, two-toned cars would be seen opening and discharging women and children, all girls, or boys deemed too young to work with their fathers. You would see us greeted at the yard gate, then led on the ceremonial walk through the flower garden.

This is the monthly meeting of the Sunny Circle Home Demonstration Unit. I walk behind my mother on the narrow path, lined with big granite rocks that Dale and Velma Rickard haul back in the trunk of their Plymouth each late September, when, after the winter wheat is planted, "We finally get to take a vacation," Velma says. "We go fishing at Estes Park. He fishes. I relax."

"I wish Harold would give in and take a vacation," my mother says. "But no. He's just sure the whole place will collapse if he leaves for more than a day."

"Well that's Harold for you," says Opal Seaman. She is a round woman, and a little stern. Her own husband, Bill, got a taste for travel in the Navy, though they can seldom afford a vacation, the way my family could if Dad weren't so tight. That is the subtext, but Opal is a practiced diplomat. "I just love your dress, Jasmin. Where did you buy it?" Opal knows my mother made herself the brightly colored, polished-cotton print dress. It has the scalloped neckline that Mom's been fond of for the last two years now and the full, eased skirt. Opal works half-time in town at the ASCS, the federal agency that oversees crop support payments to farmers. This job away from home grants her an unusual worldliness; she's accustomed to ruffling, then smoothing all sorts of feathers.

I follow behind my mother, admiring her turquoise heels, the toes round enough to kiss, and her stockings, which have a tantalizing straight black seam down the back. *Soon, I will be wearing heels,* I tell myself, and I can barely wait. My mother is among the prettiest of this dozen or so women, each wearing her finest for the others. Her figure is trim and her skin still soft and pale. Some of the women are rail-thin, while the ample flesh of others is fallen, hanging from their underarms, collected in sagging paunches under navy-blue or brown, acetate-print dresses. A few, like Opal, are large, tubular women, neckless, chinless, the typical absence of smiles more frightening in them. They pour their amplitude into straight skirts and cap-sleeved blouses, the customary attire of the demonstration unit. Their stride is mincing in the confining skirts. The wind ripples the thin fabric of the women's clothes, and some hold their hair as if, dressed for town, they've actually become town women, unaccustomed to the weather of a western Kansas afternoon.

My mother insists we wear nice clothes whenever we go anywhere. Today, I have on a print dress blooming with morning glories. The fabric enchanted me when I first saw it in Twila's two weeks ago. Now, like all the dresses my mother makes me, it doesn't live up to the sophisticated look I had in mind. The low slung waist with the narrow, violet belt is supposed to cling seductively to my hips. Except I have no hips. "Oh Julene, look at this one!" Mom says, lifting the face of a huge, burgundy dahlia for me to admire. "And those poppies!"

I smile, pretending awe over the ragged, blowing scarves of pink, yellow, and orange.

"These are about all the flowers I've had this year," says Velma Rickard. "Lost the earlier ones."

"Oh I know," says Melva Younger, "the hail stripped my garden bare." Those women whose gardens survived the storm make mental notes to bring Melva some of their canned beans and tomatoes. The Youngers live close to the bone in a basement house, dug the year they were married, the upper floor never completed, as Bob had promised Melva it would be. Melva looks twice her age, her skin wrinkled and loose on her bony frame. The Youngers have five kids, "all living in that hole," my mother often says. Three of them—Junie, Alice, and Todd—are here today. I try to act ladylike, which is to say, tamped down, controlled, as I exchange glances with them and the Seaman kids, Dawn and Bryan. We are all shy amidst the promenade of women, but that will change as soon as our mothers convene their meeting.

Stepping into the house, the women pat their hair and say, "My gracious! That wind!" and settle into the recently vacuumed and dusted living room. They blossom among the mint-green furniture, their perfume floral. I love Velma Rickard's drapes. They have huge vines over a gray background. Yellow bamboo shoots weave squares behind the leaves, and the big windows in this newer house frame a gorgeous lawn, where the sprinkler is running.

After all the women are perched on the folding chairs that circle the living room, I leave to change out of my dress in the pink, and black-tiled bathroom. I run my fingers over the cool squares, breathing the scent of rose soap.

I figure we'll have about an hour and a half to play. Normally the women hear a short talk on some domestic topic—pressure cookers, the food groups, or garden pest control—but today they must plan their fair booth. Farm safety was last year's topic. They decorated that booth in green and yellow crepe paper to match the model John Deere tractors they borrowed from their younger sons. One they displayed having overturned in a ditch, a pair of denim-clad legs sticking out from underneath. In another scenario, a rare male doll lay on the ground behind his tractor implement, a blue, fold-down disk. The women had painted his chest with red fingernail polish. I'd always wanted one of those disks to pull behind a toy tractor in the yard dirt, and I ogled it with a pang of regret over being a girl, ten going on eleven, too old for such playthings. In my favorite scene, a tinfoil lightning bolt pointed at the head of a third farmer, still driving his tractor. Across the top of the booth, stenciled letters read, "The 3 C'S OF D-isaster: Carelessness Causes Casualties."

Outside, I feel set free, wearing last summer's faded pedal pushers, a plain white sleeveless blouse and canvas sneakers. We older kids forget our dignity and dance an energetic shuffle with the little ones. I don't even mind the wind today. We are all so excited that we can't decide what to do first—investigate the kitten nest in the machine shed as Wanda Rickard wants to do,

run through the yard sprinklers, climb to the roof of one of the
neat, green-shingled outbuildings to point out our own farms
and the grain elevators in Ruleton and Goodland, ride the tire
swing over the hayloft, or, as Todd Younger suggests, play strip
poker in the windbreak. Junie and I object simultaneously.

"Todd!"

"Gol!"

"Yuck!"

A couple summers ago, I taught Todd and Junie the game,
which my brother Bruce had taught me. But I chickened out as
I began to lose, just as I had with Bruce. My parents say Todd is
slightly retarded; that's why he still comes to the ladies' parties,
although we share a birthday and I know he recently turned
twelve. I'm still astounded that he doesn't know any better than
to announce our shame to the entire neighborhood. Hasn't he
noticed the bumps on Junie's and my chests? Or perhaps he has,
and that's why he wants to play. The thought makes me shudder.

We opt for the lawn sprinkler, then a dirt clod fight in the
windbreak, which has been recently plowed. We threaten each
other with captured granddaddy grasshoppers, smearing their
tobacco juice on each other's arms. Wanda Rickard, who hasn't
changed out of her dress, and who has a habit of pressing her
rhinestone-studded glasses against her nose, coyly slips away
before any of these rowdy games begin. Every so often, I
glimpse her standing on the porch, pretending not to notice us.
She'll be starting junior high in the fall, I then remember.

When a sixth sense tells us it's time for refreshments, we
tumble into the house and struggle to contain our energy, to
stand politely behind our mothers' chairs. We expect the usual
boring questions, but also look forward to receiving the attention of so many civilized and orderly women. Instead of turning to us with the customary indulgence, they all gasp and
begin to laugh. Opal rails, "Dawn Margaret Seaman, what sort
of lady have I raised? You get your little behind back out there
and stand under that garden hose. Bryan, you see that she does

it, and when we get home, it's a lickin' for you, letting your sister get all filthy!"

My mother, less inclined to public remonstrance, says, "Julene, you need to wash up too." I'm mortified. How had I forgotten who I was, who I was becoming?

Melva merely looks at her kids, not expecting much one way or the other. Velma Rickard says, "Wanda, go onto the laundry room porch and get some towels." I look down at the dried mud on my calves and arms. I'm too big for these pedal pushers, and my hair, which Mom combed back into a jaunty ponytail before leaving home, must now be straggly and windblown.

But once again outside, I find the hose bath thrilling. Prim Wanda administers our redemption. She stands in the grass in her patent leather shoes, raising and lowering the nozzle, giggling like a little girl. I'm not even bothered knowing that Velma, Opal, and my mother have come out on the front steps to be sure we don't get mud on the towels that, unlike any of ours, match. Then Mrs. Rickard brings us refreshments—apricot nut squares and Kool-Aid. I pick the coconut off the cookies and toss it in the evergreen hedge beside the porch, feeling lucky that we didn't have to undergo the usual interrogation, girls asked if we've been helping our mothers this summer, Bryan and Todd if they've been helping their dads, if we're ready for school to start yet, or if we're entering anything in the fair. I can visualize the women inside, tipping their coffee and nibbling the dessert off the transparent, pink-tinted china, handed down from Velma Rickard's grandmother, for whom there was a big funeral last winter. "Will she really whip you?" Wanda asks Bryan.

"Nah," Bryan says.

"Might," Dawn says hopefully.

Although laughter would often ripple through the living room during refreshments, the women weren't very good visitors as a rule. After the dessert was praised and the dishes stacked in the kitchen, they would sit politely on, but you could see that they did so uncomfortably. The business meeting completed, they could barely tolerate idle minutes within another woman's domain. They folded their arms across their stomachs or rested their chins against their knuckles. The talk was almost painfully trite, and my mother would drift out of the conversation, her eyes staring into the distance as she dragged her thumbnail over her lips. Excited to have the rare opportunity to play with other kids and to be somewhere other than our farm, I couldn't understand her anxiousness to get back home. I would beg to stay another half hour and she would sometimes defer, but reluctantly. "I've got to put supper in the oven," she would say.

Over that supper, re-ensconced in her own house, Mom would tell Dad the latest news from the neighbors. Behind each woman's name—Melva Younger, Velma Rickard, Opal Seaman, Violet Roder, Vona Price, Mable Leonard—lingered the image we conjured of their men—Bob Younger, Dale Rickard, Bill Seaman, Paul Roder, Wilmet Price, Raymond Leonard. With each of these men, we associated a plot of land and the characteristic way he farmed it—straight or crooked rows, weedy or clean, cloddy or smooth, planted on time or late, good stands or poor, to the road edge or just to the telephone poles. About those men he most respected, my father would say, "He's a doer." For Bill Seaman, our nearest neighbor, he had a modicum of respect, because, whatever else his failings, he "does get out there early."

Billy had been in the Navy and had fought in World War II, while my dad took advantage of the farmer's exemption, a subliminal bone of contention between us and the Seamans. Having been places myself now, I suspect that Bill Seaman's life on shipboard gave him a glimpse of other cultures and liberated him from the conventions of his neighbors. He stripped down to his boxer shorts and white Navy cap when he drove his tractor hot summer afternoons. If Mom was planning a shopping trip to town, Dad would say, "Close your eyes when you drive by the Seamans, Jasmin. Naked Billy is sowing wheat."

Women were judged by how well they kept house, and by their own appearance. In both cases, the adjective of praise was "well-kept." To be fat or to have, as my dad often said, "a rear end as broad as a barn" was a sin in women, whereas men's heft and grooming were seldom referred to. If, when my father visited a neighbor's house, he saw newspapers and clothes strung around, dishes still on the table mid-afternoon, lint in the corners, or cats up on the counters, my father would exclaim after he left, "Gawd! What a trash heap," referring not just to the house, but to its wife. It never occurred to him to be ashamed of the way he kept his own shop. His worthiness was judged by another standard.

The men were as oblivious to raising kids and to putting meals on the table as the women were to the preventative maintenance on tractor engines, but the women rested in the lap of the men's world, not the other way around. Without husbands, quite simply, the women would have no food to serve, no home to demonstrate, no car to drive.

Even though I disliked the way boys, men, and their work were deemed superior, even though I gave voice to the rebellious notion that I would myself do the most esteemed men's work someday, as a nuclear physicist, astronomer, or vet, and even though I got good grades in all my classes, including science, the actual practice of these occupations was inconceivable to me. Each would involve the use of alien, complex tools. There would be huge cyclotrons, observatories, or austere operating rooms. Aesthetics wouldn't figure into the picture at all. There would be nothing to decorate; even I would have to dress unbecomingly. The notion of atoms fascinated me, but the elements they make up, the whole exterior world of substance and power beyond the domestic, belonged to men. Perhaps I could apply myself, understand, and succeed, but those occupations really seemed foreign and uninteresting. As a vet, there would be scalpels and formaldehyde and ether and unforgiving responsibility and manure and saliva and fleas and filth. I didn't really want to be a vet or physicist or astronomer, I just wanted to be able to say I was one. And I didn't truly want the responsibility associated with earning my own living. I wanted the luxury of womanhood, but without the lower prestige.

I was preparing to be a housewife, despite my disdain for that term. I laughed when my cousin Judy showed me, on her bed at home, how she had learned in Home Ec to fold the sheet under the mattress in crisp hospital corners. I had a philosophical nature, wondered about religious issues, was disturbed by political injustice, but it never occurred to me that I might make a living through thought. I had no models of this; no academics lived in my community or anywhere nearby. Even though I talked about college, both Judy and I knew that my real purpose there would be the classic one, for women.

During the weeks following the hail, my mother must have slept poorly next to Dad, that powerful man who had lost his wheat and feed crops. By day, he responded to his losses with goals and purpose. My mother steadily prepared and put nourishment before him. But it wouldn't be until next summer, with another crop maturing in the fields, that he would sneak into the kitchen again, after washing up on the work porch, and swat her bottom as she stood rolling out biscuit dough at the kitchen counter.

Mom had planned a trip for that fall, a vacation in Arkansas, where my father's sister Alta lived. "Oh, we won't go now," she said, as school approached and I began to wonder where I'd stay while they were gone. Mom longed to get away, to do something fun. As far as Dad and travel went, though, he was like my horse Queenie, who would choose some common object to shy away from. The hail provided a righteous-seeming excuse. Yet by October, the winter wheat would all be in the ground, the sheep would still be out to pasture, and the hail had left him no feed to cut. "We could go if he really wanted to," Mom said.

Her energy abandoned her that summer, and she took advantage of her prerogative to rest between routine chores. "I'm so ti-i-red," she would say, the end of the sentence sliding down into the depths of baritone complaint, a last vestige of the Carlson drawl my father teased her about and which she'd worked so hard at abolishing. She would lie down on the couch in the living room. "You should take a nap now too," she would say, and I would sit for awhile in the prickly easy chair and watch the lines of light along the outer edges of the venetian blinds filter through the curtains. The threads in the sashed, white, fiberglass drapes glimmered like translucent tubes. Beneath her need to rest lay an assumption about the physical frailty of women, as compared to men, a frailty I could also choose to give in to, but I resisted. The living room waited. The blue-glass coffee table. The olive-black screen of the Zenith TV. The plaster of Paris collie that I'd ridden when I was two.

The house ticked, and finally pushed me outside. I wandered the farmstead, where most of the animals were also drowsing. Penelope, my favorite cat, lapped at the water dripping from the window air conditioner unit onto the ground in Mom's hollyhocks. I picked her up and kissed her head. She dangled mutely. Overhead, clouds floated by. I trailed sticks along the walk, a circuit I'd followed a thousand, million times. I'd been doing it since long before I was six, when I marched up and down the walk with dead Christmas trees, or stalks of dry dill plant, singing "Onward Christian Soldiers."

Sometimes, when my mother slept, I would gather the energy to catch and saddle my horse. The enterprise required much effort. First, I had to go back inside, tiptoe up the stairs and pull on jeans and boots. In the barn, I filled a grain bucket with oats and carried that and the halter as I climbed the corral fences. I trundled out into the huge pasture, the grasshoppers clacking, the sun firing the part in my hair. I caught Queenie, if she was in the mood to be caught. Back in the barn, her tail flicked me along with the flies as I got the saddle down off the stall divider. I completed the cinching, the bridling, then led her back out into the afternoon.

I rode her down our road, bordered by REA power poles on the left, telephone lines on the right. Magically, out of nowhere, I could hear a radio station playing tinny music, and every so often an announcer—just the cadence and tone of his voice, never distinct enough for me to pick out words. Looking over my shoulder, I watched the house's chimney bounce until it disappeared behind a hill in the road. That real chimney, I noted, was not red, but orange. It was not charming, like the one in my set of Lincoln Logs, and the house beneath did not constitute a shrine, nor a future to long for. It was a box. For the moment, it held only my mother. In the distance, in a world that seemed frighteningly empty to me, a world I was trying to figure out how to animate with my own energy, tractors crawled over the fields. I could hear their engines below the voice of the phantom announcer.

So much was farmed in Kansas, so much plotted and aligned. Even the silence had human voices in it. But I could pretend for awhile, with my mother asleep behind me and my brother Bruce among the men in plow traces beyond me, that I was as wild as the weeds, as wild as the rattlesnakes and badgers that burrowed into the ditch banks, that like my brother Clark, who had escaped the farm, I could choose who I would be.

Reaching Down

In the dream, I'm stooping in tumbleweeds that have drifted against the prefab tin garage south of our house. It's summer, and I have that dual perspective common to dreams, in which I can see as I normally do while also seeing behind me. Over my shoulder, the close-napped buffalo grass pasture stretches toward the low place we called the lagoon. The prickly pear is in bloom, the flowers yellow and waxen, and blossoms of delicate apricot mallow totter in the wind above dusty green leaves. The lagoon is filled with water.

I reach down in the weeds along the garage's foundation, attempting to retrieve something that has blown there, or something that has been lost. I'm looking for a normally inconsequential thing, discarded or dropped. I'm not sure what it is, but the search is freighted with importance and I persist despite the thorns.

Waking, I check my hands for scratches. Eerily finding none, I recall the emptiness of that childhood landscape. I could always feel the presence of people there, who seemed to have simply vanished. Now I understand this feeling derived of my family's history in that place. The ghosts of a clan watched over our enterprise. Many of the clan members still lived, residing in town or on nearby farms. On occasional holidays, this family would manifest itself. We would gather for dinners in the big house built by my grandfather, my mother's father. But no gathering lingers as vividly in my memory as the one we had at the lagoon, the week of my tenth birthday.

It was May, 1959, and a couple mornings previous I had awakened to a thrumming, voluminous chorus of toad song.

The chanting pulsated, hoarse and male, and seemed to echo off the dome of the sky. Apparently, the far-off lightning Dad and I had watched from the balcony the night before had moved over us while I slept, bringing rain. Then the toads had come, appearing from nowhere. In the morning, I opened the screen door and stepped onto the porch. Looking southeast, the direction of the noise, I saw that the lagoon had filled with water.

Mom came out the door behind me. "Listen to those silly toads!" she exclaimed, happy and amazed.

"Was it a gully washer?" I asked.

"No. It was just a nice big rain. Didn't you hear the thunder?"

I'd heard nothing, and the lightning the night before had given me only the vaguest premonition. Distant electrical storms had become a common sight on those dry evenings, nothing more than the arid planet's tossed off electrical charge.

With rare spontaneity, my parents decided to celebrate my birthday with a party at the lagoon. Birthdays normally went by without too much fanfare—a gift, of course, and a cake shared by the family—but the annual party my son and all his friends consider their due would have seemed overindulgent in that time and place. The neighbors and our family remember the lagoon party still today, not because of a little advance in the life of a girl, but because it marked the end of a drought. Years later, my father would tell me that the late fifties were worse than the thirties. Farming methods had improved, and we avoided another Dust Bowl. But livestock was sold off and crops withered. Apparently we had some pretty close financial calls, but my parents must have reserved their worried discussions for well after my bedtime, for it wasn't until I was an adult that I realized the times were dire.

So here are these drylanders, a people whose skin, speech, mien, and humor are so arid you'd think if you cut them, sand would pour out. Here are these drylanders wading through the mud at the edge of the lagoon. Normally the valley is dry, and our sheep graze there, chawing on the sedan grass my father plants. Curly dock and redroot amaranth grow along the edge. But today even the tallest weeds are submerged. My father has owned the fourteen-foot boat so long that the sun has blistered the turquoise paint on its wooden seats. He has taken it to Bonnie Dam, a reservoir on the Republican River about thirty miles from our farm, only a few times in my ten years. He says he loves to fish, but is also notorious for never taking a day off, not even a Sunday.

Here he is, though, in his striped overalls and his gray derby-style work hat. He's pulled overshoes on over his Red Wings and the buckles flap at the top where he hasn't bothered to fasten them. That's how cavalier he's being. Wading beside my hulking father are two uncles—Raymond, balding at thirty, and Johnny, the heartthrob, a shock of his thick, brown hair falling into his eyes, which are blue like my grandmother Bair's. The rest of the Bairs all have brown eyes. Uncle Raymond, walking his characteristic shuffle, allows his side of the boat to drag the ground.

Aunt Bernice and I stand together, watching. Her husband Carrol, who was a mailman in town, has recently died of lymphoma, and she is beautiful standing here, beautiful as always. Bernice lives alone now with her daughter Dian and son Doan in the little pink ranch-style on Broadway, just one block off Main. I've always envied Dian her town parents—her mother's brown-eyed stylishness and amber, smooth skin, her father's square chin and movie handsomeness. "What do you say, Sis?" Uncle Johnny calls. His voice sounds natural and intimate out here, absorbed by miles of grass and young wheat. It is as if we've all been dropped, in the nakedness of our personalities and dress, onto the plains from which we draw our life and breath.

"Sis" is an uncommonly warm form of address in a family that recognizes few emotional ties, but Johnny will give Bernice his special attention for years to come; he'll remember her loss when other siblings begin to criticize the way she keeps house, the way she raises her kids. My father and his brothers and sisters are a haphazard lot, born to parents who counted on the oldest kids for farm labor, while doting on the youngest, among whom Bernice and Johnny are two.

Bernice replies faintly, with some gathering of heart and lips that comes out sounding all m's. "Mmmm." Silence intercedes. Then she murmurs, "Johnny."

But he's too deep in mud now to notice. "Oh-ho there, Captain Harold," he says, stabilizing himself by grabbing the gunnel. "I think we're going to have to carry it."

Dad tosses his hand up to signal my brother Clark, who has been backing the trailer. The pickup doors open, and my teenage brothers turn in their seats, take off their boots and socks, and throw them in the bed. Their jeans rolled up, they wade through the mud to the boat. Because they're young and agile and male, they do the work, unstrapping the boat from the trailer. Then they carry the heavy stern end, with the five-horse motor, while the three men carry the bow.

Dad begins walking toward the so-called lake without giving my brothers time to balance the load.

"Jees-us Christ!" Bruce complains as he sprawls beneath the boat.

"Get up! Get up! Get up!" Clark grunts, barely able to hold his side up while Bruce scampers out on his hands and knees.

Clark drops the boat in the muddy water. "Typical," Bruce mumbles, returning to get a new grip. "It's suicide.... Uhh, grr-ugh!" He makes a big display of lifting the boat. He's wearing an old work shirt that's been washed fifty times and has the sleeves torn out of it. He is Hercules momentarily. He runs, splashing through the shallows. Clark and the humbled men, left with no choice, follow awkwardly.

Having been promised a turn in the boat later, I watch from shore as Dad pulls the starter cord a dozen times. My uncles and brothers offer various suggestions.

"Flooded."

"Choke it."

"Get the starter fluid."

"Nah, ether ruins gasoline engines."

"Did you ever watch how he starts the station wagon cold mornings?"

"Yeah, but he shouldn't, causes knocks."

"Knock, knock."

"Who's there?" Clark says sullenly, certain Bruce will upstage him as always. This is his first spring visit home from college, and I am giddy to have him present. I don't realize that I'll only see him for a few brief days and then he'll be returning to summer school. He'll complete college in three years, take a teaching job in eastern Kansas, then leave soon after that for a job in Madison, Wisconsin.

"Ether."

"Ether who?"

"Ether he gets that engine started or he's going to remember this boat has oars, and who do you suppose'll get that job?"

Once the engine catches, Dad sits down without any gesture or remark, as if he hadn't experienced a moment's doubt. This display of faith in engines baffles me; if they don't work at first, they will be made to work. Resting his hand as confidently on the tiller as he does on the steering wheels of his tractors, Dad conveys the boat out to sea. On the other two bench seats, my uncles and brothers sit facing different directions, their shoulders hunched against the spray. A cloud has momentarily crossed the sun's path, muting colors so that the men remind me of New England fishermen in a jigsaw puzzle I once put together.

I'm still trying to understand exactly what it is that seems so different about this day—other than the party and the lagoon. Then I realize, it is the air itself. It is unusually humid out, and even though it's early, the sweat is already making rings below the armholes of my lavender blouse.

Hearing the low purr of another engine, I look up to see that Uncle Leonard has driven through the pasture gate, bringing Grandma Carlson on a rare visit out from town. Dad calls this grandma "Lizzie." Whenever I hear her referred to in this way, I think of the orange-speckled lizards that dart between the soapweed out in the north pasture. The sandstone ledges are so rugged there that we call the place "the canyon." I can see Grandma's silhouette behind the window glass—her forehead and chin angled backward, as if pulled by the strands of her gray-streaked hair, which she still somehow manages to wrap in a tight bun.

Uncle Leonard uncoils from the driver's seat of the green Plymouth, a car that has taken on the odor and codgerly personality of him and Grandma. It's strange to see this town car parked in the ruts of the pasture trail. It usually sits in Grandma's garage, or tools slowly, under the aegis of Uncle Leonard, down the paved streets in Goodland. Uncle Leonard doesn't work anymore; he just lives at Grandma's, freeloading off her, Dad says. He pulls the Plymouth in the drive once a week, washes and waxes it.

We are a people who devote a good portion of our lives to the care and maintenance of cars. Every male among us owns his own wax kit and chamois. On Sunday, the day Clark arrived home from college, he made it his immediate business to wash the family car. He used Coca-Cola to remove grasshoppers from the chrome bumper of our red and white Ford station wagon. I got to help, the radio blaring out the open windows. When I dropped my rag in the gravel, Clark hung the old ribbed-cotton undershirt on Mom's yard fence and hosed it off. "Splish splash, I was taking a bath, all on a Saturday night," he sang along with the radio, swinging the hose wide, getting me all wet.

"Hey!" I yelled. I ran around the front bumper and grabbed his wrist. He let me pin him on the grassy slope above the drive.

"Okay, okay!" he shouted. "Mercy!"

But I demanded he say the password. He was laughing silly

by then, but eked out "click-click" the way I used to do when I was little.

"Oh dang," I said, just as he used to do. "Gotta let you go. You opened the lock."

I don't run over to greet the new arrivals, but watch my mother and her sister, Aunt Ruth, fuss over the aged queen. I've been wading, bucket in hand, with my cousin Dian and the neighbor kids, Bryan and Dawn Seaman. We must have about a hundred toads splashing and thumping in each of the old red lard buckets my mother has given us. Cousin Linda, Ruth's tall, skinny daughter, has held back from this pursuit, and approaches the car now in her shorts and her outlandishly long, outlandishly clean, outlandishly white legs. She's wearing saddle oxfords and bobby socks. She's always gone along with every program, while I prefer the Bairs, who don't go to church and make tasteless jokes. As kids, the Bairs all raised at least a little hell, Dad says.

It's a rare windless afternoon, and the absence of wind gives the moment a sort of magical aura. My birthday. Gifts and cards piling up on the grass beside the food tables. And the rain, of course. "If we could only get a little moisture," Dad said last week. "A half inch would be a God's plenty." And now it's rained three inches. The lagoon is full, something I've never witnessed, although I've heard family stories of past floods. The treeless plains that stretch two hundred miles to the Flint Hills east of us and two hundred west, right up to the base of the Rocky Mountains, these plains whose aridity and expanse make us who we are, have taken on a new, green, softer appearance. It's as if the family also has transformed into people with leisure to play and the civility to celebrate a child's birthday.

Uncle Leonard stretches, standing beside the car. Tall and comically lean, he wears suspenders to hold up his shapeless khaki pants. He has on a flannel, long-sleeved shirt, though it's eighty degrees out. He squints and puts his hand over his eyes as he looks at the sun-silvered lagoon. The water could be clear, like a mountain lake, not muddy like it really is. Out in the middle, Dad has completed a figure eight and cut the motor, and they're bobbing in their own wake. Bruce's voice carries over the water as he murmurs the standard Bair joke about the Carlsons. "It's Uncle Lennnn-naaarrrd." Laughter. It strikes me as strange that I heard him so clearly, then I remember—there's no wind.

I don't think Leonard heard though. He is generally oblivious to all overt humor, although he smiles toothlessly much of the time, and his hazel, Carlson eyes shine behind his steel-rimmed glasses, like a man's whose outlook is pleasant. But his words always gainsay his smile. "I don't knoowww," he grumbles, his pitch swooping to the bottom register of his basso voice, "what you wanted us to come all the way out heeeeerrre fooorrrr"—down again to settle like a salamander in a mud bottom. They all do it, although Mom makes a conscious effort to speak more ordinarily. Dad has teased her over the years, so she tries to complain less also.

With typical slowness, Leonard advances around to Grandma's side. He opens her door and they all stand there—Mom, Ruth, Cousin Linda, and Leonard. Our farm dogs, Snooker, Flopsy, and Rex, squirrel up to the door. "Ooh," Mom says, swatting at them. "Get away, you nasty hounds!"

Grandma's drawl floats over the buffalo grass. "I don't knooowwww how I'm going to get out of heeeerrre."

They figure out a mode of extraction, and then set her down in the wheelchair Leonard has retrieved from the trunk. They carry her over the bumpy ground and park her under the white sheet Mom, Aunt Ruth, and Aunt Bernice have strung between the sides of our two wheat trucks. Aunt Irene, another Carlson, heavyset and aging herself, has waited under the awning. She stands and moves her chair. "Oh for heaven's sake," Grandma complains, "all the bother," but when settled and staring southward, says, "Well, gracious. Look at the lagooooon."

I hear Mom tell for the fifth time how Dad has named the

lagoon Lake Lizzie. They all laugh over this, and Grandma is noticeably tickled.

"Julene!" Mom calls. "Say hello to your grandma." I tiptoe over the grass and around the prickly pear cactus, my bare feet covered with mud, toads thumping against the edge of my pail. I stop to set a toad on the hood of the shiny Plymouth. Usually, I squirm at the notion of being a girl in Grandma Carlson's lineage—how she grumbles and demands. I don't want to be like that. But now, my father's humor has embraced her in a way that unifies her with us. Today, Grandma Carlson isn't just an old lady who sits in the mohair rocker in the small white house in town, folds of wrinkled skin disappearing beneath whichever navy-blue dress she happens to be wearing. I know we're being honored by her appearance here at this sudden, miraculous lake, named after her.

Seeing Grandma out here in the emptiness—away from town and her house there, away even from our farmhouse, which was once hers—I realize she is actually the one who set me onto life. She gave birth to my mother, who in turn had me. She gave us everything, really, trusting my dad to farm her land. It was she who planted the lilac hedge that was in full perfumed bloom two mornings ago, when I stepped onto the porch and saw the sparkling lagoon a half mile beyond. "Here, Grandma," I say, offering her a toad. "Look at its eyes; they're gold."

"Julene!" my Mom says, appalled. But Grandma cups the peeing amphibian in her translucent, veined hands.

"Oh!" she says. Her laughter is a series of squawks, like the rusty-hinged grain bin door being swung back and forth. She lets the toad hop off her lap and into the buffalo grass, and I see that she wasn't frightened at all, as I'd expected. She lived among yard animals, livestock, and "vermin," as she calls anything wild, most of her life. Maybe her son John, who was killed by lightning before I was born, once set toads in her hands also. After John died, Leonard wasn't of sufficient mettle to run the farm, so she rented the land to Dad and moved to town.

The women put on the typical Carlson feed. Fried chicken, potato salad, lime Jell-O with pineapple, strawberry Jell-O with bananas, homemade dinner rolls, hand-churned butter, jam made from their own garden strawberries and from the wild plums in the hedges surrounding their houses. Mom and her sisters cook and bake as if they were born with the know-how, the way birds are born to fly or toads to hop. The function— prepare food, clean up, prepare food, clean up—is as rhythmic and certain as breathing. We gather our dishes off the tailgates of the trucks and pickups. The adults sit in folding chairs, their food bending the paper plates in their laps. Some of us kids eat on the beached boat, spitting watermelon seeds and tossing bones over the side.

I take this moment to study my cousin Dian for signs. She still smiles and laughs in a way reminiscent of Carol Channing. Her skin is still pale like her father's, not amber like her mother's. She's still two years older than me and way, way taller. Her eyes are still emerald. She seems completely undiminished. Except I know she cried for days after her dad's funeral. Aunt Edith, the heartthrob Uncle Johnny's wife, sat up with her for three nights.

Aunt Bernice isn't as good a cook as the Carlson women. "What'd your mom bring?" I ask Dian, and she lifts a Fig Newton. It's as if her branch of the family is a hybrid form of plainspeople, privy to town ways—always dressed nicely, their hair thick and sable brown. When Dian comes out to the farm, she doesn't seem quite ready for it. She's barefoot now, but she usually wears white canvas shoes, and her socks fill with stickers. Or she'll be wearing shorts and will have no jeans when we go horseback riding.

Lured by the smell of fried chicken and knowing we kids are the most likely donors, our burly black and white tomcat Humbug tiptoes across the muddy grass and jumps up into the boat. He rubs Dian's leg, smearing himself with his own scent from nose to tail. "Oh, Humbug, here, you old smoocher you,"

Dian says, handing him the leg she'd only just bit into.

"You're a pushover, you know that?" I say, thinking how odd it is to be sitting in a boat in our south pasture, and now to have Humbug wander up to us the way he does at night when we sit on the porch stoop. I've never seen one of our cats this far away from the house before. Come to think of it, I've never seen most of the women out away from at least someone's house and yard.

"Awww," Dian says, "who could resist old Humbug?" There are other cousins here also—too many to make an accounting of. The girl cousins. The boys. All in our different leagues according to gender and age. Grandpa Bair has died recently and there have been some squabbles over land. Our grandmother Bair is gone also. In a couple years, Grandma Carlson will die too, and Aunt Irene will sequester herself in her house, just the other side of our canyon pasture, refusing to speak to my mother for the next twenty years. But we seem united today, a noncontentious family, happy to be alive, the promise of big crops ahead, two days after a big rain.

Later that afternoon, Dian, wading in water that rose to her short cuffs, cut her foot on a piece of buried glass. Bernice took her into town to Dr. Renner, whose probing and stitching Dian remembers with painful clarity to this day. She describes the doctor's metal instruments digging deep within the cut while she screamed and cried. I still feel guilty that I continued having fun for hours after she left.

The sky hung low toward evening. The air itself seemed to glow violet. We watched Grandma and Leonard's Plymouth creep back up the trail and out the gate. Finally, Dad, my uncles and brothers, hauled the boat out, their voices relaxed now, their bodies, like mine, content and tired. Mom and my aunts cleared the dishes and lowered the makeshift awning, shaking out the sheets. The Seaman kids and I carried our buckets back down to the lagoon and tipped them on their sides. We watched the toads scatter, as relatives do when years pass.

There I am, in my dream, reaching down into dried weeds for a fragment of my past life. A rag maybe, one of Dad's thin, ribbed undershirts, dropped when washing the car with Clark. Or the bottle Dian cut her foot on. While the buffalo grass plains reach to the sky beyond. After years of exile from Kansas, after I divorced my first, city husband and began living in the world alone, there came an awakening. The sun rose on an interior night, and I learned to reinhabit distance and space. I learned to care for my relatives, who, like the lagoon and toads, had seemed to materialize that afternoon of my tenth birthday, from nowhere. Where did that expanse wedge itself in the intervening years? Where did my family live? Within my cranium, in an unmapped region of my chest, or within some valve of my heart itself?

Inside Spaces

One winter afternoon when I was seven I watched as my father climbed a stepladder in our farmhouse's upstairs hallway and removed a panel revealing the attic. I gaped past the big X seams in the back of his overalls to where his head disappeared into darkness. I didn't know his purpose—perhaps he was checking the roof for leaks—but I wanted badly to crawl up the ladder and take a turn looking. He wouldn't allow it.

That night in my sleep, I traveled out my bedroom door into the hallway and up into the space. Birthed through the attic opening, I stepped across sky to those few places our family had vacationed—a pueblo in New Mexico, where a hunched, blanketed Indian sat outside a dark doorway; San Diego harbor, where I'd ridden on a flatboat beside my father; a narrow blacktop in Arizona, where, according to family legend, my brother Clark had pulled me out of the way of an oncoming truck. These places and people appeared and disappeared effortlessly, as if I were riding, as I had on just one occasion, the escalator in the big department store in Denver, watching all the splendor move past me. The sky itself seemed the agent of the movement and the visions. The blue opened out not just from our house's ceiling, but from the part of me traveling there, a core that was dormant in the daytime.

The blue wanted me, and I bloomed into it, its breadth and depth becoming my own. That was the strangest thing—at night, in my inelegant, pine-floored bedroom, with eyes closed, I dreamed a sun-lit, yawning sky. The sky was the arid, crystalline western Kansas one under which I spent my days. While sleeping, I awoke to the most prominent feature of the world I lived in, but its mystery intensified when framed by the square attic opening, as if infinity could be housed.

    We were a sky-gazing family. How could we not look skyward often on the Plains? My father, standing on our house's second-story balcony, watched over the windbreak of elms as storms brewed in the west. They rolled toward us all the way from the Rockies, bearing both the promise of moisture and the threat of crop-leveling hail or high winds. Even when there was no weather brewing, the sky presented itself as the dominant feature of our landscape. All light and distance, no trees or mountains obscuring our view, its occasional sparse clouds would seethe and unfurl. My mother, hanging clothes on her line, or hoeing weeds in her flower beds, would often stop in her work to proclaim, "Oh Julene! Look at that one." We stared up at the underbelly of a lizard, its giant, long-toed feet stepping over us, or at the muscular arm of Thor, his hammer held aloft.

Mom was particularly attuned to sunsets, which were stunning and dramatic on those evenings when clouds churned in the west. "Kansas has the most beautiful sunsets in the world," she often said. Having been few other places, she had little evidence to go on, but I believed her, and concur still today. The spectacle was easily as dramatic as the one above Moses in Sunday school pictures when God inscribed the tablets in Exodus, only number two in the Old Testament chapter order I had to memorize. The Christian religion, which I shared with my mother then, told me that God lived in the sky. While I could never thoroughly envision a cloud-walking afterlife, I did feel that it was in that direction that all the interesting mysteries lay. I wondered if, after death, invisible to everyone below, I might step over the clouds, revisiting every lost moment. Perhaps nothing good was ever lost.

Those days when the sky blazed most gloriously, my dad had the most to fear. When separate rays angled toward us through the massive cumulus, lighting his wheat fields as if in blessing, the sky might actually be preparing to wipe him out with hail. Perhaps this irony had struck my father, for he was a nonbeliever, while my mother, with us kids in tow, drove twenty miles to town every Sunday in order to attend church.

Yet it was Dad, a graduate of college Ag School, a fan of science, an empiricist, who introduced me to the most spiritually enticing notion of my childhood. After suppers, we would often stand at the front fence, craning our necks to gaze at the stars. Venus would be first to pierce the deepening blue, but a legion soon joined her. Dad explained infinity to me, a puzzle which I lay awake attempting to unravel many a night. How could the universe go on forever? How, on the other hand, could it end? What would come after? Nothing? How could there be nothing? Thinking these thoughts disoriented me. I felt as if I were floating on a fraying tether above the farm. I imagined myself expanding, looming until, perilously, I filled the universe, obliterating everything in it. Then I shrank dizzily to minuscule, feeling myself on the verge of erasure. I bloomed and shrank that way until I had to turn on the bed lamp, get up, and stare in my dresser mirror just to solidify again in my own real size.

Each morning, daylight returned around the edges, then over the top of the barn that loomed out my east window, reaffirming the existence of all that had been there the day before. On summer mornings, the blueness of the sky combined with the clarity of the night-cooled air, filling me with vivid promise. One particularly fine June morning when I was twelve, I set myself the goal of riding my horse Queenie all the way to St. Francis, twenty miles in the opposite direction of the more familiar Goodland, where I went to church and school. As I traveled north in Sherman and then into Cheyenne County, the land began its rugged descent into the Republican River valley, the buffalo grass plains now dotted by yucca and sage. I dreamed of arriving in town under my own volition. How

wondrous it would be after all those miles of virtual desert to
hear my horse clip-clop over the pavement and to have the town
kids, in their clean shorts and playsuits, look up at me from
green swards of well-watered lawn, their soft skin exposed
under the overarching elms. I would move past them in my
dusty denim and cowboy boots, having pierced a barrier into
another dimension—another county, another climate, another
life. Adding to St. Francis's mystery was an event that had taken
place there when I was seven, under the care of our family
physician, Dr. Walz.

My parents had driven me to his office one winter night
because I claimed to be suffering from terrible abdominal pain.
In fact, I was suffering from what felt like a lack of love. I had
sat for seeming hours on the bottom stair in our hallway, outside the bathroom waiting for my turn, while my father continued his bedtime shaving ritual oblivious to my full bladder. I
wailed about this until I embarrassed even myself, at the sup-
posedly dignified age of eight. When I finally got my mother
and father's attention, I affected the only pain I could come up
with that seemed equal to my complaining. Dr. Walz diagnosed
appendicitis and told my parents that the offending organ
would have to come out.

I lay in the St. Francis hospital bed that night after my parents left, feeling ashamed of the serious attention I had gar-
nered for myself. How dire the consequences I had put in
motion! I debated whether I should confess to my mother in
the morning, but there was no authority wiser than Dr. Walz.
Perhaps I really was sick. Perhaps my appendix verged on erupt-
ing. When he'd pushed at my stomach, I thought I did detect a
wee pain.

After the operation, Dr. Walz announced that he had found
an infected white blister on my appendix, which he had put in
a jar of formaldehyde should any of us wish to see it. On that
second night, the darkness was ether-doped, blurry, green-
tinted. I lay alone in the new, clean-sheeted bed, having spent

the last several hours puking bile in the recovery room. Whenever I closed my eyes, I envisioned my appendix floating in fluid on the oak shelves behind Dr. Walz's black x-ray machine. A nurse came in and asked me if I needed to throw up again. I said I was feeling woozy but didn't think so. She opened the curtains, but I turned my head away, afraid to look out. I watched her white cap and shoes as they fluttered out of the room. When I finally braved a glance out the window, I expected to see nothing—no lights, no stars, just blackness. It seemed I had pried myself loose from reality. The stars were there, I found, but to only slight relief. There was surely something else my lie had altered. Would my parents come back the following morning? Would there be a home to return to, or would I discover I belonged to no one?

As I rode toward St. Francis four years later, I pushed my hand under my belt and fingered the scar left by the appendectomy. Dr. Walz had used metal clamps instead of stitches. Remembering these, my mouth filled with metallic-tasting saliva just as it had as I'd lain alone in the dark hospital room, probing gingerly back and forth over the white tape and gauze. Maybe I could make up for the lie, which still haunted me, if I could reach St. Francis. I wanted not only to penetrate the boundary between my farm and that slightly exotic town, but to join the two worlds. Doing that would restore my faith in the solidity of the universe. But as the sun waxed larger, the likelihood of reaching my destination waned. The rays beat down on me as Queenie clomped along the gravel.

At noon, I came to Sand Sentinel, a country church, which, my parents told me, people still attended. Fifteen miles from St. Francis and only a discouraging five from home, I tied Queenie's reins to the church's antique hitching post, pulling the leather tight and doubling the knot for fear of being stranded. The building was white clapboard, the gravel lot beside it grown up around the edges in yellow-blossoming sticker weeds. I took my sandwich out of my saddlebag and ate on the church steps. Afterwards, I grabbed my apple from the bag and walked behind the church to look at the cemetery.

Handsome red and yellow brick gateposts formed entries on two sides of the little plot. Honoring the single strand of woven wire that pretended to complete the boundary between the prairie and sanctified ground, I opened and stepped through the silver-painted wire gate. The wind caught the gate when I didn't latch it correctly, and it banged against the brick pillar. I refastened it. Rubbing my apple, silently red and smooth, not at all unsettled like the wind, over my lips, I walked, the way children were not supposed to walk, alone among the Cheyenne County dead.

The graveyard was too neat for the day, too neat for the region. The ladies' club caretakers sought to civilize death. The buffalo grass had been mowed, and the north and west borders had been planted in round cedars that, standing no higher than my knee, didn't make for much of a windbreak yet. Big, polished stones marked lives made small by the elements, small like mine felt just then, as wind and heat drained the blue from the sky and the day of its promise. The pretense of the marble distanced me more than distance itself, which yawned beyond the cemetery in all directions. Wooden crosses seemed more appropriate, or mounds of sandstone.

A child bored by sanctity, as in church, and bored by the past, I had to force myself to walk slowly and read the stones, to pay the respect I knew death demanded. I recognized some of the surnames. These families had been my father's neighbors when he was growing up. Most of the dates bracketed births in the 1800s and deaths well into the 1900s, but when the gaps were narrower, I knelt and ran my hand over the engraved numbers, trying to feel the significance of death, to believe in it. Beneath the Eggers family stone lay Mae Lynn, 1895–1914, Beloved Wife of Albert. A couple markers gave the military rank of young men who, I deduced, had died in World War II. Embedded in the ground near the Loomis headstone, an embossed metal plate announced the death of Nathan, 1959–1960, just the previous year. I didn't know Nathan's parents, living, as they must, on the other side of the county line from me. I hadn't heard of their tragedy, yet virtually a neighbor, the infant Nathan had died while I lived. The scar in the earth was still ragged, touched only by scattered blades of returning buffalo grass. Instinctively, I tucked my fingers under my waistband and traced the ridges of my own bumpy scar.

I stood up, feeling dizzy in the heat. Across the road, a meadowlark sat on a fence post, throwing his complicated song onto the wind, which grabbed it and sent notes trailing across the cemetery. Did Nathan have a window, like the one I had in sleep, onto sky? Mom's religion claimed he did. But Dad, who had given me the gift of infinity, paradoxically negated eternity, saying we were "no different from jackrabbits." He clapped, mimicking a rabbit's instant death on hitting a car bumper, then threw up his hands. "Dead when we're dead," he said.

It was only six years later that I married—very young, at eighteen. My husband and I, like many others in our generation, headed for San Francisco. I never noticed the similarity in names between the town in Kansas and the famous city, but I traveled to San Francisco the same way I'd traveled to St. Francis the night of my appendectomy, under the power of a lie. I didn't love my husband, although I convinced myself I did. Believing in my marriage, in the city's glamour, in my new, supposed freedom, I painted the bedroom ceiling of our first city house sky blue. But the sky I'd dreamed had been translucent, and couldn't be captured in paint. Our ceiling turned out flat and opaque, a barrier, certainly no outlet on the universe.

Like many migrants, I had yearned to escape stasis and a dull-seeming past. But my long absence from Kansas, intended to liberate me from bondage to family and land, taught me that I couldn't live happily in a state of permanent release. I found I could reach all the beyonds, all the magical realms joined by the

infinite blue, but I longed more to be held to the earth than to
fly free of gravity, even if being held slowed my progress to
incremental hoof clomps.

I grew up under the influence of Christianity and its sky
god, always enchanted by ethereal distance and defining the
ideal afterlife as release from earth. But now, in my middle age,
the dirt my mother's hoe stirred up—rich-scented, wormy,
cool—seems as much a miracle as the sky she pointed to. The
sky in that attic dream enchanted me because, safely harbored
within the blue and miraculously still alive, were favored memories of my deepest attachments. To my brother, my father, and
the earth itself. Among the places my dream returned me to was
an Arizona two-lane highway where my brother had rescued
me. Clark will always reach out to me over that narrow strip of
asphalt in front of the low-lying motel. I, in the green dress
with the teddy bear pocket, will forever begin to cross, destined
for some object of childish fascination. Clark, with his butch
haircut and his good, white town shirt open at the neck, will
step wide onto the road, his arm extended.

That heroic brother who saved me from a truck died himself years later, under the wheels of a lumber truck. I have never
wondered if his life were exchanged for my own. I don't think
that the forces at work in the universe value one life over any
other, but such coincidences do lend reality a strangeness similar to dreams. They cause me to suspect that there is such a thing
as eternity for us, a fusion of space and time wherein events
crystallize and interrelate.

We call the reality we experience in dreams "heightened"
because the strangeness is ultra-convincing. The images linger in
memory, landmarks potent with meaning, The other two places
I visited in my sky dream are still floating within the housed
infinity of my unconscious. Were I to dive into sleep from just
the right angle, I could find myself in the upstairs hallway of our
farmhouse once again. I would float back through the attic opening, reentering that sky world, where the flatboat forever tours

the blue waters of San Diego harbor, blowing its big horn for the pleasure of its passengers. I forever stand at the rope rail beside my father, in his dapper fedora and his good wool jacket, which scratches against my shoulder as he pulls me more securely to his side. And the New Mexican Indian drowses eternally against the rectangular black doorway in the stucco wall. The darkness of that doorway seems impenetrable, but could be it is just another opening, another passage through which my brother, my father, and I are destined to travel.

If sky is release, then dirt is connection—our lives and deaths on earth in bodies among people we know. When we buried my brother in the cemetery in Goodland, I sat in the honored line of family below the funeral director's awning for the first time as an adult. I couldn't believe that my brother was being lowered into the earth, and I returned the next day, as if to verify. The awning was gone, rolled up and stored, no doubt, on the aluminum poles that had supported it, destined to be re-erected over another plot in another part of the cemetery soon, like a circus big top reappearing in a nearby town. All that remained from the day before was a mound, chunks of buffalo grass sod. I knew that these would grow together as the earth contracted and expanded with moisture and sun. I knew that eventually the scar would be healed over, but in that moment the wound was new, and I probed it.

We have only scars, in the earth and our own bodies, to prove we lived. At the same time, we are more than this. We are a marriage, earth to sky. We eat and love on earth, breathe and dream in sky, yet all functions require the cooperation of the other element. I think of sunlight and chlorophyll, oxygen and green plant life, clouds and lakes. Not only does matter lift and float in sky, but sky enters matter. Somehow all that we experience lives within. I don't know where my sky world will go when I die. I don't know where I will go. Mom says to heaven. Dad says to earth. I don't wish to live in either place without the other.

Beacons

I turned down another party invitation recently. I couldn't justify hiring a babysitter. Not because of the cost, but because Jake had been in daycare all week, and I had two evening classes. Amy, a fellow teaching assistant who shares my office in the English Department, thought I should go anyway. "Do something for yourself," she said.

"Where do you think most parents are on Saturday night?" I asked her.

I knew the night of the party would proceed like most. I would read to Jake and play with him, then, after putting him to bed, read a novel assigned in one of my classes. Across town, my childless, mostly younger friends would talk about the book. They would know about the literary period, the author's other work, the critics' opinions, and I wished I could share in that conversation.

After several minutes of silent paper grading, I looked over at Amy. "Besides," I said, "being with Jake is for me. We are a family, and if I can't take him to a party, I'm not going."

One of Amy's eyebrows lifted, but she refrained from commenting. I remembered then, as I so often do, how it was when I was little. Every other Saturday throughout the winter, we traveled to farm neighbors' houses for card parties.

Eight families belonged to the club. Their houses were landmarks on the Kansas prairie. On summer nights, I could see their yard lights clearly from our front fence. The realms lit by those lonely beams were as inaccessible to me as the stars. Then, on the first Saturday night in November, we groomed ourselves as if for church, but with more flair.

Dad's aftershave mingled with the scent of Mom's powder in the chill air inside our station wagon. I was the youngest, and sat bundled on the front seat between them. We were always at least five miles down the road, the snow streaking at our windshield, before Dad turned on the heater fan. I held my Buster Browns up to the vent and basked in the warmth flowing up my white tights.

Snowflakes shimmered like rings of Saturn around our host neighbor's light pole. We stomped our feet and entered the overshoe-cluttered porch, the odor from work clothes threatening our well-soaped scent and sheen. Hearing a muffled chorus of voices, I would shove my coat at Mom, throw open the kitchen door, weave through a forest of stockinged legs and high-heeled pumps, and run up the stairs to where the hosts' children held court over miniature John Deere tractors, Easy Bake ovens, canisters of clay, slinkies, crayons, and coloring books. Our parents interfered with us only when our screeches and thundering feet penetrated the din of their own games and gossip. My dad has told me he gave me a spanking once for being too rowdy at a card party, and he was chastised for it by Faye Blue, a teacher in the one-room country school my cousin Judy attended.

"That oughta do some good," he said to Faye as I walked off, crying.

"Maybe it does you good," she spit back. Whatever damage he did me that night, I am none the wiser today. My boisterous pleasure so outweighed the punishment that I don't remember it.

The fifties were hard times for farmers, with grain markets down, and never enough moisture. Getting together after two weeks of little but work and worry heightened the color on the cheeks of even the poorest, most stoic farm people. Jokes traveled from card table to card table, sending waves of laughter around the modest living room. Shouts punctuated the steady

chatter whenever someone succeeded in shooting the moon.
The men rubbed their wives' knees and bluffed their way
through ten-point pitch as if it were five-card draw. The women
leaned back in their chairs and let out enormous hoots, their
faces shining through their powder.

Outside, the snow continued to fall, blanketing the miles of
dark prairie that lay between our houses. The big kids helped
the little ones into snow pants, and we burst from the house like
popcorn jumping from a skillet, the snow cushioning our
shouts as we ran through the drifts. By the time we came back
inside, the hostess would be serving refreshments. The kids
drank punch usually, but at some parties I was allowed to sip
coffee from a delicate, transparent cup, just like a grown-up. I
lifted the cup from its matching saucer proudly, even though it
contained only enough coffee to tint the milk. As the adults
handed out prizes for the highest scores and a booby prize for
the lowest, I wandered off to the hosts' bedroom. I fished my
mother's coat out of the tremendous pile and burrowed beneath
it, letting its caress usher me to sleep.

The few times I've taken Jake to parties and he's
gotten tired, I've wished he would simply nestle into a comfortable bed full of coats as I used do. But his exhaustion has
never been the honest tiredness that comes when kids run
themselves down in play. The only child present, or one of only
a few—tolerated by people who are my colleagues, not neighbors—he grows cranky. At two, he quickly lost interest in the
toys I brought for him, then squirmed out of my lap as I
attempted to bounce him. Now, at almost five, he wends his
way through the crowd, charming the adults with his penchant
for conversation, but returning to me often, his cheeks black-
ened with chocolate frosting from the brownies he's been
snitching off the dessert tray. Pumped up on sugar from both
this source and the punch bowl, he asks, with increasing impa-
tience, if it's time to go yet.

Whenever I've tried to get him to sleep at a party, I've had to lie down with him. Pent-up in the darkness of a back bedroom, laughter beckoning from the hallway, I've counted to well past five hundred, waiting for his fidgeting to stop. Rarely has he succeeded in going to sleep, but, when he does, his peace then enchants me so much I've lain on beside him, content to listen to his breathing and watch the rise and fall of his little chest. I only wish to share his childhood with others. I wish for us to be part of a larger community together.

I wouldn't feel this yearning quite so strongly if I had a mate. This is a simple desire I've been unable to satisfy to date, but it is complicated by a strain of logic that my dignity requires I mistrust. When I was growing up, I had two aunts who divorced their husbands and one whose husband died. It was generally agreed among our family and farm neighbors that these women could not succeed at raising their children, especially their boys, alone. They were accused of spoiling their sons with too much tender affection, too much regard. As if I weren't already sensitive on this issue, my parents nudge me with our family's aunt lore. I am exhorted to get on the ball and find Jake a father.

I respond by pointing to articles in the news weeklies in their own magazine rack. More and more women are raising kids alone, some by choice. I show them stories about women who visit sperm banks. I don't admit to my parents how I yearn for Jake to feel the security I did during those winter car rides, nestled between two parents. Nor do I confess my guilt over how much I depend on their generous financial help. With that and my teaching assistant's salary, I avoid the fatigue and virtual hopelessness so many other women raising children alone experience.

Yet I've also found inspiration reading about women who are less financially fortunate than I. In Gloria Naylor's The Women of Brewster Place, I encountered heroines who rang truer to me than those crafted by male authors, in the classics. Madame

Bovary and Anna Karenina neglected their children for men, then romance let them down. Naylor's women, members of the black subculture in which, according to my parents' *Times*, over half the families are headed by single mothers, centered their lives on their children. They made families between them, filling the emptiness left by absent fathers.

　　　　　My man left me when I was two months pregnant. Like many of the men in Naylor's book, he got by on good looks and charm. Marrying him was the dumbest thing I did in all the years after leaving Kansas at eighteen. Today I tell myself I married him because I had reached the age of biological crisis, the do-or-die age for potential mothers. But that first summer back on the farm you couldn't have told me that. I longed for the man, not the child.

Broke and humiliated, I did all I could to earn my keep, driving tractors throughout most of my pregnancy. Dwayne's scent hung about me, despite the dust the farm implements stirred up, and despite the stink of the tractors' near-boiling radiator water that record hot summer, or the stench of the hydraulic oil I spilled trying to reach hidden spouts. I bounced across the fields in everything from my father's biggest, quietest, air-conditioned 4850 down to the thirty-year-old 4320. That tractor tore over the terrain, its engine screaming with fifties zeal. I cranked the radio on high, and let the nasal laments of the country and western singers scour my emotions. I bawled fervently, shouting and cursing Dwayne over the noise, until I saw my father's pickup approaching. Then I would clench down on myself and the steering wheel, trying to drive straight while reaching for my thermos. I splashed water on my face and wiped it with my sleeve. "How's it goin'?" Dad shouted over the noise of the engine.

"Fine," I yelled back, never mentioning the cramping that could have resulted in a miscarriage. My son did not become real to me until he was born. On that day, I touched my nose to his scalp and inhaled a scent that surmounted and replaced the memory of his father.

At first, I felt confident over raising Jake alone. I took heart from those swaggering magazine moms. "Who needs a man?" they said. I told my family I shouldn't have much trouble. I was an outdoor person. I could rebuild a car engine and remodel houses. I could teach Jake all the things men taught their sons. My brother Bruce chortled condescendingly. I couldn't tell whether he laughed out of wisdom or a mere reflex of his sarcastic temperament, but by the time Jake reached six months, it seemed to me that the only thing worse than his not having a father would have been if the one I had so cavalierly chosen for him had stayed.

The first hints were subtle, but disturbing. When my brothers visited, Jake stared up from their knees, his eyes alight as if he were seeing God. It could have been their beards that Jake found so fascinating. I hoped that was it. But the same thing happened when a clean-shaven male friend visited from San Francisco. Although Jake was very devoted to his grandpa, he seemed especially crazy about men who were the age of a likely father. Then his second word, after "hi," at nine months, was "da-da." I was taking a correspondence course in etymology at the time, preparing for the possibility of returning to college. Newly aware that words have histories, I looked up the derivation of the word *dad* and was appeased: "Middle English *dadd*, *dadde*; Irish *daid*, imitative of a child's cry." It seemed infants made the sound naturally, without attaching meaning.

By twenty-four months, though, Jake was undeniably enthralled by dads. He would flip the pages of our photo album in search of his favorite picture. A girlfriend of mine from Arizona had sent the snapshot of her husband dangling their daughter Sage by her hands, making imprints of her feet in wet cement. Jake would find the page and crouch silently over it, breathing mist onto the plastic page cover. After a minute or two of meditation, he would ask, "Sage's daddy?"

"Yes," I said, wondering when the inevitable question, "Where's my daddy?" would come.

It wasn't just Jake's overt longing that troubled me. On a few occasions he bit other children. He grew angry when thwarted and would sometimes strike me as I toted him to his room for a time-out. In analyzing this problem, I focused on my own inadequacies. Did Jake need the love of a father to curb his aggression, a sparring partner to take it out on? As a woman, was I just ill-equipped to discipline him properly? Was my voice not authoritative enough, my love too clearly unconditional?

I felt as if Jake and I were a skewed atom, missing an electron. The balance just wasn't right, and the isolation was nearly unbearable. During this time we lived on the farm my father owned—in the house he and my mother had lived in when they were first married. They'd sold the Carlson place, where I'd grown up, and moved to town years before. Although my father came out to work each day, Jake and I spent our nights alone.

Mercury vapor lights were the new technology on farms. They came on with the dark and extinguished themselves at dawn, the light they cast icy blue. Jake and I stared at the distant blue beacons of neighbors and I felt as if my childhood were replaying itself, but with a new, coldly eerie tinge. The card parties still took place in the winter, and the women's club my mother had belonged to before she and Dad moved to town met year-round. Although I remembered the club meetings as being tedious, the conversation stultifying, I felt lonely enough to imagine myself attending. I was considering a future for my son and myself as farmers. The gender roles, although still in place, were not nearly as strict as they'd been in my childhood. Many of the neighbor women did farmwork and would not reject me on that score. I wanted to sit among them, lifting coffee to my lips as my child played with neighbor kids. But although I'd hinted, no invitation arrived for me to visit the Sunny Circle Home Demonstration Unit.

I yearned even more to attend the card parties. Laughter

rang in my ears as I stared over the plowed fields in the direction of my neighbors' yard lights. I could still feel the warmth
inside the otherwise winter-enshrouded houses. I wanted my
son to grow up with the neighbor kids and for myself to have
a place, however quirky, in local society. I'd made many attempts
to socialize with my neighbors, but couldn't bridge the distance
between beacons without a farm husband.

Now I am a graduate student in a writing program at the
University of Iowa. My decision to come here was spurred, in
part, by the inaccessibility of the farm life I remember from
childhood. Confused by my conflicting desires, on the one
hand, to live that life, and, on the other, to escape it, I now write
about it. Jake and I go home to Kansas only during summers.

Our lives in Iowa City were difficult at first. Jake
cried every morning when I dropped him at the day care center. The director held him up to the window to wave. I made
faces at him, blinked my car lights, and honked my horn—all in
hypocritical glee, for I felt just as anxious on separation as he
did. Then at night, with no one else to interact with, we were
too fused. How many block towers could I build for him to
demolish, how many nursery rhymes could I read him, how
many games of peek-a-boo could I play without the respite of
adult interaction?

Meanwhile, his fascination with fathers crescendoed from
"da-da" to "DADDY!" He clung to the men who worked at our
day care co-op, often competing with other children for attention from their fathers. At two and a half, he asked it. "Where's
my daddy?"

"Somewhere in California, I think, Honey. I'm not sure
where." Whenever he played airplane after that, he flew to
California.

My work as a student, teacher, and mother left little time for
dating and the potential discovery of a mate. I did go out with
a couple of men—older, returning students like me. Neither

appealed to me enough to pursue a relationship, yet due to Jake's obsession with fathers and my own training as a Kansas daughter, I allowed myself to entertain the notion. "Boys especially need fathers." This was the message coming from my parents as well as the media. Although the news weeklies recorded the trend toward unmarried women having children, their pundits attributed the rise in crime to single parenting.

I resented the implications—that Jake's relationship with any man I found for him would be more important than his relationship with me. Only a man could raise a boy right, only a father could prevent him from becoming a criminal. And I resented how Jake's relationship with that father surrogate would have to pass through me. Would I wind up martyring myself, uniting with someone I didn't love in order to satisfy Jake's quest for a dad? All this while, Jake's real father was oblivious to him. The few calls I'd had from him demonstrated his continued alcoholism and that he wanted only to renew his primarily sexual relationship with me.

Returning from a summer in Kansas for a second year of school in Iowa, I couldn't face the isolation of our apartment. I took a financially unjustified risk and rented a house with extra rooms. Then I ran an ad, "Wanted, housemates." Jake was three. I fantasized that some man might call who could provide the missing ionic charge in my little family's lopsided atomic structure, but no such person showed up. The two or three young men who did look at rooms were uninterested in Jake, while he fell instantly in love with them. I turned away those candidates with a sad regret I was hard-pressed to explain to Jake. Living in a male's presence without male love would have been like living at sea without fresh water.

Women also called, but lost interest when they heard the details. None relished the idea of rooming with a toddler and his mother in a family neighborhood on the outskirts of town. Jake and I had our own problems adapting to the neighborhood. He was unaware of suburban property lines—invisible yet indelible boundaries. Every afternoon, on coming home from the day care center, he grabbed Allie, his duck on wheels, and rumbled down the sidewalk. I followed, tugging Rex, a puppy I had adopted from the pound. Jake would abandon Allie, and I would catch up to him just in time to thwart his conquest of a more appealing mode of toddler transport.

"This is our house," one child informed him, and tried to unwrap Jake's fingers from the handle of his army-green mobile strike force tricycle. Jake leaned down unceremoniously and bit the kid's arm. Mortified, I carried him home kicking and squealing, with Rex's leash looped around my off-wrist and Allie's "brain post," the wooden handle that ran ear to ear, slipping from my grip. Such acts on Jake's part failed to endear him to the other mothers on the block, with whom I had only that much in common—motherhood. With a friend, I could have compared notes and searched for the cause of Jake's biting and discussed ways to curb it, but Jake and I were new to the neighborhood and now suspect. I imagined the neighbor women recounting the day's incident over their dinner tables, behind doors that I feared were permanently closed to me. From my increasingly alienated vantage point, I felt that their airtight marriages formed boundaries as unsubtle as the chain-link fences in each backyard.

Nan arrived in the nick of time. She was a graduate student in art, looking for an inexpensive room. "Do you like kids?" I asked. "I mean Jake isn't always an angel."

"I love kids," she announced, giving Jake an impish grin. "You wanna do a flipping truck?"

"What's a flipping truck?" I asked.

"I'll show you." Nan positioned Jake, willing and curious, in front of her, grabbed his wrists from between the backs of his legs, and flipped him over forwards.

Jake let loose a barrage of squeaky giggles. "Again," he said.

I rented the other rooms out to a divorced mother and her eight-year-old daughter, but these two spent most afternoons and evenings at the mother's new boyfriend's house. It was Nan who did me the most good. Tall and athletic, her hair short-cropped and curly, she often championed Jake in her airy voice, which squeaked when she went up the scale for emphasis. When I told her, in tears, that one of the neighbor women had declared her driveway off-limits to Jake because he had gotten too rowdy and accidentally overturned a flowerpot, her dense-ly freckled face broke into a sympathetic smile. "Illegitimi non caborundum, Julene. Don't let the bastards grind you down."

"He doesn't mean to do anything wrong, but, you know, he did bite a little boy once."

"The biting is just a stage, Julene. He'll get over it." Finally, there was someone around who loved Jake, not as much as I did, of course, but someone who would reassure me, as a hus-band might.

"How am I going to explain to him he can't go over there, when that's where all the kids hang out?"

"Don't prevent him."

"Don't?"

"Don't. It's her problem. Let her embarrass herself, picking on a three-year-old, if she wants to. But stand up for him next time. It's you she doesn't approve of."

"Me?"

"You're different. She probably wonders why you're raising Jake alone. But she'll get used to you."

Nan was right. Gradually, Jake and I won tenuous accept-ance in the neighborhood. We were not invited to any barbe-cues, however, or parties. Outside my home, my social life, in Iowa City, depended on the fellowship of other grad students, who didn't have kids. The Unitarian church I went to for awhile had a nursery Sunday school, but seldom staged a social event for both parents and children.

Nan, like my teaching assistant friend, counseled that I should get out more often. Why didn't I join her for dinner at the new Japanese restaurant in town? I couldn't, not with a three-year-old, I told her. "Bring him," she said.

"I'm not sure Jake can handle that. I don't suppose you'd want to go for cheeseburgers and malts at the Hamburg Inn?"

"Nah. Maybe some other time, Julene." Nan had a way of using my name often, as if I would remain, despite her kindness, a stranger forever. It was Japanese and company for the evening or another night alone with Jake, building block towers.

Discreetly, I asked the waiter to seat us at a corner table. Jake fidgeted waiting for the meal, but this mattered less to me as the sake began to take hold.

When the sushi finally came, it was delicious. Jake didn't think much of it, but we got him a bowl of rice, and since I let him put his own soy sauce on it, he was pleased. Nan and I had several laughs trying to show him how to use chopsticks. Then, engaged in our own conversation, we didn't notice Jake scooting off his chair. When I looked around, I discovered him peaking over the edge of another table. The woman seated there said, "Boo!" and Jake fell to the floor in a fit of giggles.

Leaning out of my chair, closer to Jake's level, I tried to beckon him back to me without causing a scene in the quiet restaurant. "Jake! Shh! Come back here."

Jake said "Why?"

I looked apologetically at the woman and her husband whose meal he was interrupting. "You don't bother other people when you're in a restaurant," I said in as loud a whisper as I dared. "Come back here. Now."

"Why?"

"Come back and then I'll tell you."

He began to do his frog imitation, hopping back to our table. I scooped him up and set him in his booster chair.

"Why?" he asked again.

"Finish your rice, and we'll see what they have for dessert."

"But why? Why can't I talk to people?"

Just a week before Jake and I had gone to the reservoir to

throw sticks for our dog, Rex, and had seen a parent slap her son and shout, "Don't 'why' me, goddamn it!" At the other extreme would be a parent who tolerated bad manners without giving any correction. I wanted to find the happy medium, which lay, I believed, in the direction of clear discipline backed by an explanation. But I had mixed feelings on this particular answer and sat for a moment in contemplation.

Nan reached out and touched Jake's arm. "People come here to have private time together, Jake. You're supposed to stay in your seat and eat your meal. Don't bother strangers."

I was grateful for Nan stepping in. This was exactly the kind of reinforcement I missed having. Children were supposed to stay in their seats, but the incident cast me back in the longing mode again, where I was wont to travel. On my own rare trips to restaurants as a child, I had enjoyed gushing attention from my parents' friends and neighbors. There were no strangers in my hometown.

I ordered Jake a cookie for dessert, then I held him in my lap, trying to get him to settle down while we waited for the check. Finally I gave Nan some money for my part of the tab, and too soon for me, but not soon enough for Jake, we were out of there.

Almost. Jake was fascinated by the waterwheel at the door. A foot bridge spanned a little pond, its bottom sprinkled with pennies. I didn't have any change, so I sent him back to the table to ask if Nan had any. He dashed off on that mission, and I remained crouched on the foot bridge, joyful and a little tipsy, reflecting on my good fortune—a happy child, a new, steadily closer friend, a stomach full of excellent food.

Someone said, "Ma'am." I looked up to see a portly man in a three-piece suit. He stood at the door, an overcoat draped neatly over his arm.

Once certain he had my attention, he stated firmly, "Ma'am, if you can't control your child any better than that, you should-n't take him out in public."

The only response I could muster was to stare. Where had he been sitting? I hadn't noticed him.

"I mean it," the man said. "You spend money for a nice dinner, and it's very disturbing."

I looked through the door he held open onto the portico, where stood his dinner partner, probably his wife, for the couple had a settled air. She nodded, and, backing her man, affirmed, "It truly is."

Having said their piece, they made their dignified exit. I wandered, dazed, back to the corner where Nan sat searching her wallet for change. I repeated the couple's remarks.

"Non caborundum, Julene. Illegitimi," Nan said. "It's their problem."

The busgirl shook her head with regret. "I'm sorry that happened." She and Jake had flirted off and on all evening.

Despite these assurances, I cried driving home that night. I sensed such disapproval frequently even if it was seldom voiced. It unsettled me most because it conflicted with my own childhood. I still had the card party model, in memory, a vision of the way things ought to be. Didn't children, like the adage said, belong to the world? Jake needed that world more than most kids, because he was so social, and because we were not enough, just the two of us alone. Yet whenever we ventured out of our rented ranch-style house, I cast him, naturally outgoing and unsuspecting, into unwelcoming hands. Instead of the Faye Blues of my Kansas childhood, adults who would speak up for him were I to discipline him harshly, we fell under the scrutiny of disapproving strangers. The aura of judgment sometimes did cause me to act harshly. Even though the neighbor woman had already swatted Jake's bottom and sent him home bawling, I made him help me sweep up every last grain of dirt from that broken pot— this while he wailed and I tried to conceal my own tears.

Gloria Naylor's women, though living in poverty and confronting different problems, had the wealth of spirit and good sense to find their solution in each other. After Nan moved in, it seemed that my social experiment, to which I'd resorted in desperation, was beginning to work. I had the companionship I'd longed for and Jake had the benefit of instruction and love from at least one other adult.

Our budding happiness was threatened, however, when I received a call from our landlord. We had the ill-fate of being flanked by cranky neighbors. To the north of us dwelled a fifty-ish couple, who had once cut Rex's tether line because one end of it was tied to their fence and who had Nan's van towed because she left it parked on the street for more than two days while opting to ride her bike to class. They had now contacted the zoning commission and reported that our house was over-occupied.

I studied the letter the landlord had given me, then dialed the number on the letterhead. The secretary was sympathetic but said nothing could be done. The neighborhood was zoned R-1, meaning a maximum occupancy of one family plus one renter. We were technically two families—we two mothers and our children. Plus Nan. If I asked the other mother and her child to leave, not only would that cause them hardship, but the rest of us would have to move as well. I couldn't afford the rent without subleasing at least two rooms.

I felt sickened by the prospect of moving back into an apartment like the one I had rented the year before—outside of town, in order to accommodate Rex. There would once again be no one to talk to nights.

"Okay," I said to the clerk. "But I was just wondering…"

"Yes?"

"How do you define family?"

"Well you and your son are a family."

"Yes, I know, but what if a man and a woman were living in the same house and they both had kids? Would they have to be married in order for them to meet the definition for the purposes of this ordinance? Or sleeping together? I mean you guys don't send spies around, do you, to see who sleeps together?"

The woman hesitated, then said "no" with a curious, uplift-ed curve on the "o." She was getting my drift.

"So what if? I'm not saying this is the case, but just what if we were two lesbian women living here, two women with chil-dren who were making a family between us, and we were rent-ing out one room? Would that meet the ordinance's require-ments? Because if it didn't, that would seem like a clear case of sexual discrimination to me."

"Just one moment," the clerk said. "I will have to ask one of the commissioners about this."

While I waited anxiously for her to come back on the line, I contemplated the irony in what I had just said. I was not a les-bian, but Nan was. The other mother didn't know this, and she would have been appalled at the insinuation I'd made.

The clerk returned to the line, her voice triumphant. "You have won your case!"

I hung up the phone and leaned back against the wall, shak-ing with relief on my own behalf, and rage on behalf of other single mothers who might also be trying to reinvent their lives, but who didn't have graduate degrees or teach English. What chance would they have against the officious certainty expressed in a zoning commission letter? The incident hadn't left me unsullied either. I felt shame over my rushed but careful choice of words—*I'm not saying this is the case*—and the distance I had put between myself and Nan. By worrying that the clerk might think I actually was a lesbian, had I not crossed into the camp of my neighbors, who could tolerate so little diversity that they had mounted a campaign to rid the neighborhood of a quiet group of female renters?

Last year, the mother and her daughter moved out and two new, unrelated housemates moved in. As far as I know, our neighbors to the north are unaware of the fragile argument that spared us, and they haven't re-instigated their complaint. I'm not sure how I'd dodge it this time. These two

new women, along with Nan, Jake, and me, have created a sem-
blance of family. I had two evening classes this spring. Nan took
Jake to her studio on Mondays, where he was more than happy
to make art. On Tuesday nights, he frolicked with Laura, a twen-
ty-two-year-old comparative literature student, who treated him
as she would a younger brother, playfully teasing him whenever
he whined. Our third housemate, Rose, a veteran day care work-
er, taught him songs and let him play dress-up in her room.

We had additional luck in Joe, the husband of a friend in
my writing group, who offered to be Jake's buddy on the night
of our weekly meeting. But Jake is less fascinated with Joe than
with Laura, whom he now declares he intends to marry.

I would like to think this means that Jake's desire for a father
is less intense, but I know better. Jake is four and a half now, and
just a few months ago, I made the mistake of answering too
candidly when he asked, "When is my daddy gonna come,
Mommy?"

"Well, honey, it's almost as if you don't have a daddy. You've
never met him, and he's never met you, and ..."

Jake's eyes were instantly red and brimming. "I have a
daddy!" he shouted. "I do too have a daddy!"

In the aftershock of such moments, I have contemplated
writing something to warn off those women considering
sperm banks or other alternatives. *You don't know what you'll be getting into. You may not need a husband, but your child will need a father.*
Naylor's women didn't choose to mother their children alone.
They simply made the best of the circumstances their disappearing men left them in. I try to imagine what it would have
been like if my mother and I had been alone in that car back
then. She would have been driving, instead of Dad. It would
have taken a lot longer for the heater to warm the car, with all
that empty space to fill. I can't even picture our destination. It
would not have been card parties. As a single woman she would
not have been invited to those. As a single woman, she would
have left the farm. She would have searched, as I am doing, for

an alternative to the life she'd been raised to lead.

While there is no doubt he feels deprived in not having a father, I remind myself that my childhood wasn't perfect either. I clung to the front fence on many a night, watching yard lights blink off as kids, who were only rarely my playmates, went to bed. Remembering this is difficult, because the card parties offer a preferable memory, one which coincides with our society's nostalgia over the fifties.

Although Jake and I have only polite friendships in this two-parent family neighborhood, he does have playmates next door, an advantage I didn't have. And the kindness and companionship of the women in our household helps us transcend our isolation. It has been a miraculous year. But now the school year is over, and our family is disintegrating.

Last week Nan left to spend the summer in Seattle, and she isn't sure she'll be living with us again next fall.

"Nan is coming back, isn't she, Mom?"

"We don't know yet, Honey. She may need to live closer to her studio." I say this as if Nan is at the mercy of her circumstances, even though her news devastated me. How could she put convenience before our bond? The answer is too obvious and upsetting to dwell on. While I was reinventing society and redefining my notion of family and proving there were viable alternatives to raising a child with the help of a father, Nan was renting a room and enjoying casual friendships.

"Yeah, but she'll still baby-sit me, won't she?"

"Yes, I know she'll want to do that."

And Laura is packing up her things and putting them in storage. She plans to spend a year in France. "I wish Laura didn't have to go," Jake says.

"I wish she didn't either, Jake, but this is a great chance for her." I issue these assurances out of the pretense that we are a real family being temporarily separated, while I mourn the truth. We are makeshift, easily destroyed by a light wind. "Just think of all the things she'll learn."

"Yeah, like how not to laugh when people cry."

Apparently, the latest teasing session went a little far for Jake, the way it often does with real siblings. Rose gives Jake a hug. "You silly," she says. "You know Laura doesn't mean to hurt your feelings."

Jake takes her hand and examines her many pretty rings and red fingernails. "You are going to watch our house for us this summer while we're in Kansas, right, Rosie?"

"Yes, I am going to watch your house for you this summer, Jake."

"But Rex is coming with us, right?"

Rose reaches down and pats first Jake's, then his dog's head. "Of course he is," she says, lacking the heart to tell Jake that in the fall she is moving in with her boyfriend.

Laura, Rose, and I huddle in the living room and talk after Jake has gone to bed. We talk about his model behavior of late and how he's grown. We exchange the addresses of our mothers and fathers, thinking if we lose track of each other we can contact parents, the only resolute ties. During the day, we are easily distracted, unable to concentrate on our work or our preparations for departure. When one of us goes somewhere, the others tag along, relishing these last few days together.

I pack for the summer in Kansas and tell myself that Jake and I will always find others to love, to lose, to replace. The best we can do is to be open and take the risks. We are really no worse off, I tell myself, than most traditional families, which can be too insular. And how often are they a sham, their nucleus a television, casting a glow as eerie as mercury vapor over an empty farm yard? We will weather the losses, I tell myself. After all, Jake's first word, before "da-da," was "hi."

The Gleaners

My father's felt derby rests upside down on my coffee table. Wearing his familiar, pin-striped shirt and his town trousers, he stares vacant-eyed from the couch. "He's farming," we used to say on such occasions in the past. His obsession with his work has long been a source of fascination and humor among us. These days, the vacancy of his stare has more to do with age. I also suspect it has a little to do with Bruce and me, his remaining children, who have failed him. Bruce was to become a farmer. I was to marry one.

My parents have driven three hundred miles up to my current home in Laramie, Wyoming, from theirs in Goodland. Bruce came with them, not just to visit me, but to get my pickup and drive it home. As the result of a complicated family trade, it is now his.

On moving to Laramie last year, I bought a big, old two-story house. It has bay windows with leaded glass and peeling exterior paint, which I am considering all means of removing—sandblasting, water-blasting, scraping with the aid of a heat gun. It has a stairway with a fir banister that, like all the wood in the house, has been kicked and abused over the years, but thank goodness, never painted.

We sit in the living room. Sit. My father's gaze is cloudy these days, no longer bright and lively like my son Jake's, whose brown eyes the family agrees he inherited from his grandfather. But occasionally Dad's humor and arrogant command resurfaces. On his first visit, he pronounced my house "Julie's folly." His taste in houses runs to the modern, and he scoffs at the nuances that I call character. High ceilings make the rooms difficult to heat, he complains, and wood-framed windows let in drafts. He is oblivious to the architectural niceties—the carved pillars separating my living and dining rooms, the dormered upstairs bedrooms. But yesterday, my brother went down in the basement and came back upstairs announcing that my Lennox was the best, most fuel-efficient furnace made. Which helped. Practicality has always reigned over beauty in my dad's heart. He sits a little less stiffly now, withholding judgment.

"Well, I like your house," Mom says, her nod accentuating the folds of skin at her neck, unavoidable despite her fitness at seventy-five. My house reminds her of the home she grew up in, the one where she raised her three children. Clark, her firstborn, died six years ago, which must have intensified in her, as it did in me, her longing for our lost past together, on the farm. She and Dad live in town now, having moved when I was sixteen. They traded our farmhouse and land for acreage nearer the land Dad inherited from his father, then built a yellow-brick ranch-style, which, like the other brick houses on the perimeter of Goodland, announced its farmer-owners' wealth and success.

My brothers had long since left for college by the time we moved to town. Clark attended summer school even during his first year, signaling he would be the first to fail my father's dream of a farming son. When Bruce came home, he toted Bob Dylan records under his arm and a comparable attitude under his hat. "How is our father," he asked sarcastically, "who art on the farm?"

Early every morning Dad got in his pickup, which dropped mud clods on Mom's oft-swept garage floor, pressed the button on his Genie garage door opener, and slowly backed out. Through the window over the kitchen table, we watched him leave, hunched in his seat, his gray work hat pressed down over his ears. He began living a kind of exile, and his conversation, which always centered on crops and weather, seemed irrelevant, although our livelihood was still crop and weather dependent.

"Oh dang it, anyway," Mom would say. "He left the garage door open again."

Now, sitting in my living room, Dad says, "That picture sure looks nice on Julie's wall, Jasmin." Together, we admire one of my mother's largest and most intricate needle-points, a reproduction of J. F. Millet's "The Gleaners." Having promised me the picture several years ago, when she finished stitching it, Mom kept it for me in her living room while I went back to school and got my graduate degrees, in Iowa. They brought it with them this trip and I hung it this morning over my tacky, homemade bookcase.

In "The Gleaners," three women gather wheat stalks from a field of stubble. Their figures are round and indistinct in long dresses, scarves, and aprons, their faces turned to the ground. Behind them, several hive-shaped stacks dwarf the other work-ers. The painting has been a favorite of mine for as long as I can remember. Wheat is the lifeblood of Goodland, and a huge mural of "The Gleaners" used to hang in the old First National Bank on the corner of Twelfth and Main. My mother once explained it to me.

We stood in the bank, breathing in the smell of money, derived from rich dirt, and gazed over the mahogany tellers' rail at the dark, awesome painting, which glowed under a coat of shellac. She said the scene was from "the old country." The stacks and the horse-drawn wagons belonged to the farmer. The women were poor tenant wives, taking for their own baking only what the landlord's machines left behind. My mother's tone affirmed our luck, our liberation, a truth I inhaled at school from the patriotic history texts and at home, roving our family's three thousand acres, a farm of only middling largeness in western Kansas. In America, people farmed their own ground. They were never tenants on others' land.

Jake, who is nine, comes into the living room carrying something in his shirt that stretches it nearly to his knees. He leans over the coffee table, a piece of used furniture I picked up back in Iowa. Our dog Rex teethed on its corners. Jake dumps out several pounds of rocks. "See my collection?"

"Well! Good gracious," Mom says, waiting for me to react to the damage he's done to the already battered tabletop.

Wishing to bridge the gap between her expectations and Jake's excitement over seeing her, I say, "Gee look at all those rocks. Why don't you show us your fossils, then you'll need to put them away and wipe the table."

Jake digs out the gray rocks imprinted by ancient fish. We picked them up along the forlorn, mucky banks of the Iowa River, where we went often during late afternoons. Now we have mountain ranges to roam over. We have the West, and we are five hundred miles closer to my parents, which has resulted in their paying us this visit.

They seem to feel less comfortable in our home than we do in theirs. This is not especially a function of my comparative poverty. Bruce's houses are always as run-down, his furniture as dented as mine, but he is married and has two kids. My parents slide into the groove when visiting him, but here they seem more worried, aloof. The discomfort derives from the fact that I am raising Jake alone and center my life on him, my occupation, and literature, instead of on a man. Mom and Dad suspect my single existence, worry that my job as an adjunct English instructor at the University lacks security, and say I'm "just dreaming" about being a writer.

Lately though, all of us are trying harder to communicate. My father is very old—eighty this year. The doctors tell us that his heart is pumping at only twenty-five percent capacity. Knowing each reunion could be our last, we try to muster wisdom; we try to be together more intensely, to make up for the past silences, to fill the past emptiness. We fail, because routine muteness has carved deep ruts in us. My parents' unsmiling stillness, whether in their house (in their big easy chairs, at the supper table, or before one of their three TVs) or at my house (their postures upright in my brown-carpeted, flawed living room) destabilizes me. I often leave their company wondering *Who am I?*—a baffling crisis in identity at my age. I can't help but think we've lost something that it wasn't inevitable we lose, something we failed to cherish, something akin to art.

My father and brother concern themselves with the nonaesthetic aspects of "The Gleaners." "How do you figure they got the hay up there?" Bruce asks.

"Well I don't know," Dad says, his voice tired.

Bruce looks more like Dad every year, his eyebrows tangling as the hair on his head gradually disappears. He wears his fringe long and curly, arousing frequent complaints from Dad. But Bruce's tone has grown more respectful in the last few years. "Did they have beaver slides back then?"

Dad says, "Well, surely not."

"How, then?"

"Pitched it, I guess. First up on that wagon, then up on a higher one, then to the top."

I don't ask what a beaver slide is, because I should know. It's always disturbed me, how little I learned about the farm while growing up. I envy my brother and father their shared knowledge, the resulting equality between them.

The conversation soon leads to farm memories. My dog Rex, who is patently uneducable, is compared to the fabled Elmer, a sheepdog my parents owned before I was born. Elmer was so intuitive my mother could simply speak to him and have him obey. "One day, I told him, 'Elmer, why don't you get me that chicken over there.' And you know what? He did. He did!"

"He had a gentle mouth, too," Dad adds. "Didn't harm the chicken, just brought it to her."

We remember other hallmark moments from our lives together, on the farm. Mom's voice lifts in pitch and affection as she recalls how Harold, my father, used to tell Bruce and me bed-time stories. "He told about horses out in that north pasture."

"Bruce's eyes would get as big as baseballs," Dad says. His voice rings with humor, as if he's remembering for the first time, as if we haven't reminisced about this each of our last several reunions.

"Clark would hide around the corner in the hallway," Mom puts in. "He thought he was too old for 'baby stories,' but he couldn't keep from listening." Hovering behind each of Mom's mentions of Clark is the last notice she received of him. Her Lutheran church minister, having been contacted by the Goodland police, knocked at the door of the ranch-style about supper time.

Down in that pool of emotion that springs from childhood, down in that charged realm that unites us in a richer past, these images swirl and surface. A green chenille bedspread and white sheets tented over my father's knees, clad in red and gray striped pajamas. The smell of Mennen aftershave. Dad shaved twice each day, once in the morning and once after a steamy bath, which softened his otherwise leathery cheeks and hands. His gray and white striped Big Ben overalls, which he called "overhauls," lay draped where he tossed them, over the rose-colored, quilted hamper, their copper fasteners dangling. The Big Bens emitted odors of various tractor oils, dust, sheep manure, and grease.

"Well, Bruce and Julie," Dad began, then, out of the side of his mouth, addressed the doorway, "And anyone else who might be listening." He grabbed my hand and squeezed it. "Did you know there's a big hole out in that north pasture? I lost my pliers the other day. Thought maybe I put 'em on the tail-gate and they fell off. So I was out there walking around looking for 'em when I stumbled over a soapweed bush and I nearly fell in that hole. Good thing I didn't, because it's about a hundred feet deep and a thousand wide.

"Well, I peered over the side and what do you think I saw, but a herd of horses. They were sleeping, because they are nighttime horses. The king of the stallions lives down there, and he's all gold-colored, just as shiny as a polished nugget. He has a star right in the middle of his forehead, and a

silver mane and tail. And he's got a mare who's pure silver. You kids think
you'd like to ride those horses?"

In my living room, Dad continues reminiscing. His voice is
full of yard gravel, just as it's always been. "I'd have you kids do
the hooves while I told the stories. 'Clippety-cloppety, clippety-
cloppety.' We'd ride to the moon, and we'd always go too far."

"Back, now, Goldie. Back up there, Silver. Whoa, now let's go down and
take a look at that crater." We loped the circumference of the moon, then
returned to the prairie, which Dad painted empty of yard lights and farmsteads, as it had been in "Indian times."

In that second story of our farmhouse, we felt a
delusive sense of permanence. Each season had its rituals. On
winter nights, Mom, in her home-sewn housecoat, would turn
the big basement furnace off and light the smaller gas stove at
the top of the stairs. The grate would turn red through the mica
front, and the metal would creak reassuringly, radiating heat
that made our barefoot trips across the floorboards less bracing.

Then, each dry June, we would throw the windows open to
the cooling breeze. Small miller moths would squirm their way
between the screens and window casements and swarm into the
house. Dad would go on a miller rampage before bed. He
would set up two stepladders below the hallway lights and place
basins of soapy water atop them. In the morning, the suds gone,
but the water fluttering with masses of dying moths, Mom
removed the bowls. I awakened to the sounds of her complaints. "Stinking millers," she would say as she carried the
basins gingerly out the upstairs door onto the balcony and
emptied the contents off the west end, where only mowed
weeds grew, not her summer-drunk hordes of perennials.

As keen on summer as Mom's flowers, I would kneel at my
east window, sun pouring over the barn opposite. I would press
my nose against the cool screen and breathe in the combined

scents of damp earth, which rose up from beneath Mom's yard sprinkler, and dust, which had collected in the trough of the window casement. Beyond the barn my father's ewes and lambs grazed the pastel inclines of our big pasture. We found arrowheads on those pasture hills, where we also had to watch for rattlesnakes, for we lived on the High Plains side of that invisible rain curtain that meanders along the hundredth meridian and marks the beginning of the arid West. One degree, forty-two minutes beyond it, but beyond it just the same. Seldom more than fifteen inches of rain fell during a year. Rattlesnakes were among the kings of that dry country, as were the coyotes, who yelped, like mortally wounded children, just beyond our windbreak. These wild creatures gave the land its fangs, and despite all our taming influence, reminded us that our agenda, in staying alive, in raising sheep and wheat, was not uncontested.

"Grandpa, want to see me shoot my B-B gun?" Jake asks.

"Ooh," Bruce says, wringing his hands and speaking in the quavering voice of an elderly grandmother. "You watch out. You could lose an eye." Grinning, he glances at Mom.

"Well, they are dangerous," Mom says, only a little perturbed at Bruce's teasing. "I read all sorts of stories every year about kids getting hurt that way."

"Hell," Bruce says, "Clark and I used to try to hit each other in the eye."

I bought Jake the B-B gun so he could experience some of the pleasures we had, even some of the dangers—under supervision. Mom and Dad were not nearly as protective of us as they are of our kids. They were even less protective of my brothers than they were of me. Driving tractors all summer robbed Bruce and Clark of late childhood. It's no wonder both chose other occupations.

"Come on, Grandpa," Jake says. "Please." I drag an old oak dining chair outside, and Dad is again seated, watching Jake plunk B-B's into a cardboard box. I stand with my hand on my father's shoulder, feeling the sun's warmth on the brown wool sweater Mom insisted he put on before coming outside—lest he catch his death. He reaches up and grabs a lock of my hair, and in the same irritating fashion I remember from girlhood, lets his hand hang from it, dragging my head to the side. "When are you going to dye it red?" he asks.

"Why should I?" I say coolly.

"Well, you can't expect to catch a man with gray hair."

"I don't want to snare one, like a rabbit. I want one to come willingly."

Dad shrugs and folds his hands back in his lap, giving up too easily in our usual repartee. I like to think my hair is an organic sun-bleached silver. It seems gray to everyone else, but has overtones in it of the same blond my mother has chosen in her tints for the last twenty years, the color of prairie grass in late August.

My mother "did" her hair before the trip. Doing my hair is unnecessary. I wash it. It dries fluffy. I stick a barrette in it and go, sometimes while it's still damp, which is the state it's in this morning during my parents' visit.

Each generation has its core values, and in our case anyway, the ideals compete. "I never would have agreed to move to town if I knew the old house would be torn down," Mom says. Yet I remember how she pored over house plans for years on end, drawing various versions of her dream house on graph paper she kept stored in the dining room buffet. She copied the houses after those she saw in *Better Homes and Gardens*.

I, on the other hand, value the antiquated over the modern, and natural beauty over manufactured. By choosing this big house in Laramie, its architecture reminiscent of the farmhouse, by scraping chapped paint from its exterior and laying on a patina of aged ivory, I hope to make my son a home as nurturing as the one my mother and father provided me. Both parents

modeled industry. Images of their work return to me in kitsch
Technicolor. Dad's red wheat trucks. His spun-gold grain fields.
Mom's cinnamon rolls. The ice cream she made every Fourth of
July from the reluctant offerings of our cow, Rosebud.

I romanticize the past while my parents have always roman-
ticized the future. It's not difficult to figure out why. Their lives
were hard. To realize any ambition, whether as simple as feeding us kids or as fanciful as a house in town, took huge amounts
of physical labor. No wonder they embraced each technological
innovation—first an automatic washing machine and dryer,
then supermarket milk and butter. Meanwhile, the age of Dow
dawned in the yard and fields.

I remember our first naive embrace of the chemical solution. As a child, I pumped DDT out of a long-tubed sprayer onto
my horses' backs. I loved the smell and feel of the cool mist as
it descended over my bare arms and the sheen when I brushed
the oily chemical into my mare's roan coat. Dad has continued
the embrace unto this day, every June injecting ammonia fertilizer through tubes into the wheat ground, and applying Treflan,
Atrazine, and Bladex to his corn, soybeans, and pinto beans, all
crops that wouldn't grow in Kansas without the aid of irrigation. He's rigged the 4010, his oldest tractor, with a chemical
spray rig, and his hired man bounces over the rough ground
full throttle with the wings extended, cones of mist tinting the
ground orange.

In town, Mom still plays out her half of the farm couple's
dedication to food production—Dad feeding the world, she
feeding Dad garden-ripened tomatoes. She also transplanted
dozens of irises from the farm, her mother having planted the
original rhizomes before she was born. But I feel ill at ease
standing with her amidst the blooms during my May visits, just
after the school term releases both Jake and me. As a child, I
took leisurely pleasure in the yard surrounding our farmhouse.
I played with the dogs there and pushed my doll buggy filled
with mewing kittens up and down the walks. Today, Mom's

lawn is chemical green; a crew from a garden service mows it once a week, after which the timed underground sprinklers begin spurting of their own accord. The property is rimmed in red lava rock over black plastic, and instead of blending at the edge into my father's domain, her town yard stops abruptly at the curb. Due to the miracle of herbicides, she is pleased not to have to contend with the stickers and weeds the way she did in the country. There, the wind lifted field dust and drove it through the windows and eaves. The new house is airtight and seldom harbors a moth. When one does appear, Mom sprays it with a direct hit of Raid.

Both of my parents seem less themselves in town; they seem drained of spirit. This has been true from the day we moved, but it's taken years of reflection to pinpoint why. When my mother stepped out the farmhouse door on her way to gather eggs or to hoe the garden, the sunlight, serenity, and space affirmed her. It didn't matter how ordinary she looked in her cotton housedress and her white anklets, an Ace bandage wrapped around one calf to ease the pain of varicose veins. She was queen of all that land. That sun and space still affirm my father as he "oozes" (his word) between his fields in his pickup, his elbow out his window, but when he goes in for lunch on the farmstead, he sits in an easy chair in the hired man's double-wide trailer house. He takes a sandwich out of his lunch bucket and witnesses the other family eat their hot dinner at table. He comes home at night as if returning to a bedroom community from a job at the factory. He and Mom can't step out the door and watch the clouds gather over his wheat fields, and on my visits, I can't take my son out to the yard fence where my parents took my brothers and me to imbibe the silence while pointing at stars.

By daylight, my father is pragmatic. He practices no faith, scoffs, in fact, at the demonstratively religious, and he has never voiced regrets over what was lost on those plains, four thousand feet above sea level, two hundred treeless miles east of the Rockies. If a couple square miles of prairie belonging to him escaped the plow, it was merely because there were too many ravines, making the land more profitable for pasturing sheep than for growing wheat. Like his father and his grandfather, he spent many spring months turning up the sod the Indians rode over. The meadowlarks frantically circled his head as his machinery ravaged their nests. Yet in his bedtime stories, he translated the meadowlarks' song. They called warnings from their perches on yucca blossoms, "What are you doing over there, young girl?" and "Watch out for rattlesnakes, you tender little morsel!" We galloped in the sky above plains that were, in my father's imagination, as yet untouched by the settlers who were his grandparents. I sometimes wonder how he can be so unconscious of the sway that land once held over him. Beauty, in my father's conscious mind, equals bucks. It equals crops. It equals bricks.

Literary scholars, I often tell my students, point to a tendency in rural writers to honor landscape by having it function on the level of character. But characters are actually overshadowed by setting in rural prose, I tell them, which is nothing short of the right and natural order. We exist in a place. That place is our creator. This soulful truth is proven on every page of virtually any westerner's work, ranging from Willa Cather to William Kittredge.

When my family moved into town, into a suburban-style house, we evicted ourselves from the place that birthed our stories. I would be simplifying to say the move detached me and began my floating electron status. I would have left the farm anyway, and not to marry a neighbor boy. I would have gone to college, would have departed Kansas for some more glamorous-seeming destiny. My brothers and I were raised, by our parents and our culture, to take what we had for granted, to feel it and ourselves inferior to what we could have elsewhere, to what we could be elsewhere. But the fact that my parents won't drive home to the farm after their visit in Laramie, that they return

instead to the yellow-brick ranch-style in the town neighborhood that's grown up around them in the form of other farmers' brick houses, robs me of the possibility of return. It's as if
we betrayed ourselves, not appreciating our own past, unaware
of how the vast, sweeping plains that surrounded our farmhouse provided the spiritual underpinning of our lives.

The land my family lived on made up for, even created, our
style of communication, which today feels inadequate. The
labor of our days, much of them spent outside, left us honestly
tired and alive of an evening without the need of too many deep
words. The silent rural personality is a stereotype; silence
descended in our family only after the move to town. On the
farm, we had our light exchanges, our bedtime stories, our
jokes and grudges, which the place that created us made sufficient. For as characters, we were secondary. We were unified in
an unannounced, unpondered love of the place we lived. The
unraveling of our story corresponds with the predictable
American denouement. We had this great open continent, this
airy gift that filled so much more than our pragmatic needs, but
we gave no credence to the nonmaterial things that derive from
land and space, the things you can't really own.

I dream of my brother Clark often. Usually we
are separated by some boundary, a reflection, merely, of present
fact. In the most reassuring dream, we are in the basement of the
old farmhouse. That space used to be dank and spidery, and I was
frightened of it as a child. It smelled of the orphan lambs we'd
nursed in one of the rooms, of the tobacco of hired men who
slept in others, of coal tar from a relic furnace. But in this dream,
the basement is clean and high-ceilinged, the concrete smooth,
the lighting bright. Clark has built himself a room out of pine
plywood and two-by-fours. He insists, from behind his parti-
tion, where he continues to saw and nail, that he is happy there.

In a far less reassuring dream, our family gathers on a summer afternoon in the rutted farmyard in front of Mom's lawn

fence. We jam all our luggage into the trunk of a brown sedan. We take off down the road on family vacation. When we get to Highway 27, which runs west to Denver, it dawns on me that Clark isn't with us. We've left him behind like some piece of forgotten luggage. Mom reassures me that he is following us in his own car, and I feel him back there, with his crew cut, his loud sports coat that he wore when he danced the jitterbug at high school mixers, his Future Farmer of America preparedness. But then up ahead, on one of the highway's few hills, we watch in horror as a big red wheat truck overturns. I know, despite the earlier feeling that he was following in his car, that he has, in fact, been driving the truck, and that he is dead. It was when we left the farm, some deep awareness tells me, it was when we left that we spilled all our dreams.

I sold my rust-eaten Nissan pickup to my brother Bruce for one dollar, this figure being a bit of folk wisdom, handed down. "Do we really have to name a price? Couldn't I just give the pickup to you outright?"

"No," Bruce insisted, standing over me at my computer as I typed up the bill of sale according to his instructions. "How many cars have you bought in your life?"

"I get your point." Bruce is notorious for the various tin buckets he's driven over the years, ever since he was fourteen and got his learner's permit.

We drove downtown to have our transfer notarized at a local bank. I tried to talk as the short blocks sped by, because I didn't want him to go. "So you should come up and go trout fishing with me and Jake this summer, Bruce."

Bruce laughed, whether at the submerged plea, the nightmarish prospect of being trapped on a fishing trip with us, or because he had too many other things on his agenda, I couldn't tell. "Yeah, well I wanted to have a little time off this spring, and I've fiddled away half a week already. Don't tell Mom and Dad, but I'm thinking of buying a greenhouse. I think I can sell winter vegetables."

My brother is a frustrated farmer. His fascination with plants even led him to major in botany at college, but Dad's drive and demands prevented him from stepping into his pre-ordained role on the family owned land. He chose instead to become a reporter for small town newspapers. "Hell," he said. "I still don't know whether to leave or not. Do you think they'll make it home alive if I head on back, or should I stay and lead them home?"

I wanted him to stay, but said instead, blandly, "They'll be okay, I'm sure." Bruce looked out his window at the run-down houses we were passing. "Sun-drenched stucco," he declared. "It's the West all right. What a threadbare existence, but people hang on. Wouldn't move to Ohio if you bribed them." Because Bruce lives in central Kansas, in a flat town that has no mountains nearby, I suspected he envied me a little, which pleased me.

We chose the First Interstate Bank. We walked up to the polished oak teller's window. Underlying that approach was a joint awareness that, despite our jeans and flannel, we had as much right there as anybody. The First Interstate didn't have the gloomy rich glow of the First National in Goodland. Plate glass let in more sun. The floor was orange carpet, not black marble. But the money in this bank's accounts came from ranching and oil, just as land-derived as our family's had been for several generations.

Having lived in cities, having been a businesswoman myself at one time, I am usually more forward in business settings than my brother, but Bruce took me, and the teller, by surprise. "Where can we get a bill of sale notarized?" he asked unceremoniously, without the courtesies that I precede my requests with. I wondered if this was because he was more country than I, or because he was male.

Upstairs in the bank's plush-carpeted offices, a well-dressed, older secretary, her definitely gray hair parlor-styled, said we didn't need a notary on the bill of sale. "I can't register the car in Kansas without it," Bruce stated when the woman pointed this out, and she acquiesced, placing her stamp over the gap between our signatures.

We drove back to the house. I knew that Grandma and Grandpa, as I've come to call them ever since Jake was born, would be waiting stoically inside, without thought to their own entertainment. I felt I was being abandoned to their "twenty-four-hour care," as Bruce had described his last two days with them.

Bruce asked me if there was anything he should know about the pickup. Still aching for a real conversation, I raised the disturbing issue that is getting old between us. We've had various discussions on the subject, all of them leading nowhere. "What are we going to do when he dies, Bruce? What are we going to do with the farm?"

"What can we do? Farm it," Bruce said. I've also heard him say, "Sell it," without so much as a blink. Those times I've objected, for sentimental reasons. But on that March afternoon, we seemed to have switched positions. I'd been thinking myself more of a realist and had been confronting boldly the notion of having my father's lifelong obsession gone, replaced by money in the trusts our parents have set aside for Jake, Abby, and Josh, our children.

We returned to the living room. As foreseen, Grandma and Grandpa had not moved from their positions on the couch and rocker. Jake had long since given up hope of engaging them and had ridden his bike to a friend's. The interior of the house was dim and autumnal, like the colors in Mom's exquisite needlepoint. The picture looked so good on my wall because it reflected the tones in the gold, finger-smudged wall paint and the scarred molding, which I hoped to find the energy to sand and re-varnish during the approaching winter. The hunched women reminded me of my parents, and of Bruce and me, of us. Ours was once the wealthy family, but now, even though we still owned the land and threshed the wheat with big machines, we'd become the gleaners. Our harvests, no matter how many bushels piled up in our bins, or how many dollars accrued in the banks, could not replenish our emptiness.

"When are you guys starting back?" Bruce asked.

"Oh, tomorrow morning."

"So you know how to go—through Julesberg?"

Mom nodded.

"Bye," Bruce said. He grabbed his duffel. They'd all stayed in a motel, but he'd brought his bag that morning in preparation for leaving.

Mom sat quietly as her son made one of his abrupt exits, but these departures over the years have prompted dread in me. Impending absences, the consequent loneliness, have driven me to each counteroffensive move of my life—out on my own, only to feel bereft at center. "I want my dollar," I said.

Bruce took his wallet from his pocket and began to pull out a bill.

"No," I laughed. "I was just kidding."

He shoved the dollar back in his wallet. And he was out the door.

I spent the rest of the day alone with my parents. Then, the following morning, Jake and I went out to the porch to wave good-bye. In the driveway, instead of my pickup, sat a brand new, red Isuzu Rodeo. The fanciest car I'd ever owned, it was Dad's way of providing for Jake and me, who have no one else, no other male, his way of being certain we're driving something practical and safe for years after he's gone. If we only listen to him, he's said often, and keep that income-producing farm he spent his life building, he can foresee our having no other problems. He insisted the car be red, the color he's always preferred in his own trucks. He also had the dealer add air-conditioning, even though I said we could do without. I won on the manual transmission, preferring, as usual, the old way over the new.

Life in Space

I've been visiting my parents for only three days, and now I'm loading my horses to leave. Lilly, my son's little dapple-gray mare, puts her nose up in the air for a moment, resisting as I tug the rope, then gives up, the sound of her hooves reverberant as she steps into the empty trailer. Too easy. After my horses have munched free grass and oat hay in Kansas all winter, I ought to earn this exit. Henry, my tall, sorrel gelding, concurs. He'd rather back up, dragging me with him, than come forward. I tap him a few times on the rump with the lunge whip, which returns him to the rear of the trailer. He sticks his nose in, snorts, drags me back again. Knowing I'm frightened, Henry takes advantage. He spooks sideways, rears, then for no apparent reason, gets in. He doesn't really want me to haul Lilly to Wyoming without him. I slam the door and push the latches shut.

My brother comes ambling out of nowhere. He's wearing jeans, work boots, and a thin blue work shirt like those Dad always wears. His shoelaces don't match. He buys his clothes at the Wally World in Hays, a Kansas town east of here, near Schoenchen, the hamlet of seventy-five people where he now lives. I doubt he even bothered to dress nicely for the trip he took a couple years ago to New York City. He did a column for the *Hays Daily News* about that trip. He wanted to turn tables on New Yorkers, who sometimes write clever essays about the interior of the country as if they were on anthropological missions into dangerous deserts. Appropriately, he wore his wicker hat, shaped like a pith helmet. "What are you hunting?" someone asked him in a bar. "Assholes," he said. According to Bruce, it was a reply New Yorkers could appreciate, and the conversation went swimmingly from there on.

I steel myself for one of Bruce's acerbic comments, but for no reason I can discern, am spared. More than that—he commends me. Nodding at the trailer and the loaded horses, he says, "You performed the miraculous."

Bruce's shoulders have taken on the rolled, muscle-bound look of our father's. He wears his hair and beard shaggy. Since he quit his job at the *Hays Daily News*, his face and arms have become sun-darkened. He now works outside, rototilling his neighbors' yards.

"It wasn't too hard," I say, feigning confidence. I wonder if he saw the whole operation. I feared I wouldn't be able to catch the horses this morning, let alone load them. Each June like this one, I come down, visit for a few days, then hitch up my rusted orange and white two-horse trailer behind the bright red Isuzu Rodeo Dad bought me after his last stay in the ICU and tow Lilly and Henry back to Laramie. Any true westerner would be ashamed to own such an un-American, clashing eyesore of a rig, but at heart I'm a plainswoman, not a westerner. My father's utilitarian blood runs in my veins just as surely as distance trained my eyes and this lofting, arid air taught me the pleasure of mornings. You can float on the air in Kansas, which laps at your skin and has a buoyancy like saltwater. It ripples Bruce's blue shirt as he grabs the back gate of the trailer and peers in at Lilly, the pony who is now my son's, but originally belonged to Bruce's daughter.

"I just stayed out of it," he says, referring to the loading. "Knew if I tried to help, the whole thing would go up in smoke." He looks in at Lilly. "Son of a bitchin nag," he says. "She was miserable when we had her."

"She's never given me any trouble."

"Oh gah," Bruce says, an unspellable expression of dismissal and remembered frustration.

Despite his arrogance elsewhere, Bruce ventures almost

humbly here on the farm. Walking the huge earth under this particular sky diminishes him to kid size, as if nothing has changed in the last forty years. It seems odd to see an adult afoot here, unenlarged by a four thousand-pound Ford pickup splattered with dried mud. No one walks in Kansas. The neighbors, along with the farm foreman and his wife, note our odd behavior, I'm sure. We are the kids who went away and come back every so often just to stay on the good side of Harold, our father.

In the past, before his visits to the ICU eroded him a bit, Dad bragged about being a "tight old bastard." He has told us often this is how he came to own six sections of dry land wheat, leveled irrigation ground, and native grass. He talks openly with his neighbors about his farm's future. The conversations focus on the absence of sons all around—sons who were supposed to mature into farmers and continue working the ground their grandfathers broke out of the sod. As examples of such defections, Dad cites his and my mother's siblings, some of whom squandered their inheritances. He then brags that he and the lawyers fixed that. Bruce and I, his surviving children, "can't touch the principle. The trustees won't let them."

"He's a sly old fox, that Harold Bair," the neighbor men must say over suppers with their wives. "Put it all in trust for the grandkids."

I've wondered what effect this will have on Bruce's and my children, who stand to inherit a farm grown even more sizable than it was in our childhood. Will they opt to tread water in jobs as no-account as ours—Bruce's as a garden tiller, mine as an adjunct university English teacher? Will they also pursue avocations as artists?

My brother and I both write. Many have remarked on this odd coincidence, that two children from a remote western Kansas farm family would grow up to be writers. Pride prevents me from confessing that I mimicked my brother in this, the same way I mimicked him in so many other things, as a child. As a star-struck younger sibling, I tried to win favor, in our parents' eyes, equal to his. But there are other reasons also, reasons impossible to explain in casual conversation.

Sometimes Dad gets surly about our choice to become writers. He says to me, "You kids would have to make better livings if you didn't have this farm to fall back on after I'm gone."

"I know," I admit.

"Well, what about me? What about me?" he shoots back. His big disappointment is that neither of us wants to take over. Dad has never wished to do anything else but farm, while Clark, Bruce, and I did. Still, his words arouse self-doubt in me. *I am nothing without my father*, goes the refrain, and I renew my resolve to succeed at writing before he dies.

I put the grain bucket and lunge whip in the trailer saddle compartment. For some reason I can hardly imagine, Bruce stays, leaning over the back door, scratching Lilly's rump. Within minutes of my arrival at my parents' house in town two days ago, Dad said, "We ought to call Bruce." Then, after supper, I overheard him talking on the phone. "You should come out. Julie's here." When Bruce arrived yesterday, I couldn't help feeling the old childhood hope surfacing, that my brother came to see me. This is the first moment I've had alone with him.

"So Dad commands and you come?" I jibed.

"No, well, I'm going to steal Mom's stuff."

"No! That kills me."

Mom has been writing her and Dad's family histories, remembering her own childhood, especially. She's not aspiring to publication, only doing the things exceptionally responsible people do before they die—recording family stories for future generations, clearing out the garage, getting rid of all the old books. Perhaps after fifty-six years of marriage, she can't imagine a life after Dad is gone, but her health isn't really in danger. It's Dad who's ill. I cast a glance in the direction of the double-wide trailer house, but my view is blocked by one of the three Quonsets. I wonder if he'll come out this morning. That's

usually all he can manage anymore—the half-hour drive, a brief
visit with Ron, the farm foreman, then the return to town. After
dinner, which consists these days of a bowl of soup and perhaps
half a sandwich, he sleeps the entire afternoon.

I look back at Bruce. He recently finished writing a book
about this place, the farm. Using the World Wide Web, which
reaches even into his unfinished basement office in Schoenchen,
he got himself an agent, who peddled the book to a dozen New
York publishers, many of whom wrote him complimentary
rejection letters. "I wish I could follow my heart on this," he quoted
one when telling me about his ordeal. "Well hell! Why don't
they!" he shouted. He then bought the Dustbooks small press
index and chose a publisher called Steerforth based on two factors. The house was in Vermont, and the editors were male. "I
figured they could relate to a farm book better than twenty-five-
year-old Jewish women from New York City. Hey, it worked."

Now he's going to plunder Mom's journal before I get a
chance to. That's what kills me. I've also had designs on her
journal. In singsong, Bruce recites what his publisher has told
him. "The absence of your mother and sister are like gaping
holes in your narrative." He kneads his hands against each other
and grins nefariously. "I look forward to the revisions. Now I
have a chance to trash horses."

He is referring to my reputation, in the family, as a horse-
woman, and I have to laugh at the crack. But I conceal my reaction to his other news. God, Oh God, Oh God, I will be a character in my brother's book rather than the author of my own.
Even if I thought that from his skewed vantage as the eternally
older, eternally wiser brother he could represent me fairly, there
is no satisfaction in being a character in someone else's book,
not if you write yourself, and certainly not as an afterthought.

I envision my brother and me coming together this morning—him from behind the shop Quonset, suspect, walking, me
loading the horse trailer in the reenactment of my continuing
abandonment of this place. How hollow the hooves sounded as

they first struck the floor of the empty trailer. My brother and I are two former citizens, come to mine the past, to observe and record the nuances of our father, our mother, the neighbors, the hired man and his wife, on this spot of earth that has not yet been rendered into a prose commodity. *You've performed the miraculous,* Bruce said earlier. I wish to achieve that in my writing. The miraculous in our calling is recreating the life of a place, of a family culture, in all its dimensions. My brother read my book last winter. Does he believe that, at least on occasion, I captured truth? Did my successful depiction win his respect? Is that why he's hanging around this morning, when generally I have to go find him to say good-bye? Or is he, as he purports, just doing his research?

We hear the buzz of an approaching two-stroke engine. My son Jake whizzes by in Ron's go-cart. "Going a little fast," Bruce says.

"It has a fouled carburetor. Stalls every lap."

"Probably all that's saved his life."

Just as Jake reappears from beyond the scraggly windbreak of mostly dead elms, the cart putters to a halt. His frustration is palpable. The puffs of smoke coming out as he pulls the starter cord could just as easily be rising from beneath the huge orange motorcycle helmet he is wearing. I'm struck by the contrasting repose of the dozens of farm implements lined up beyond him in the mowed buffalo grass lot. The long rows of machinery are themselves an eloquent rendering of our family's history on this land. The newest ones are so wide that their ends must be folded up for transport or storage. They sit with their undersides up in the air, teeth and blades bared. The older implements sink gradually into the ground, the grass growing tall around them, tumbleweeds caught in their tines. "I see they finally moved the 95's out of the sheep barn," Bruce says.

"95's? Oh, the old John Deere combines."

"Yeah. You could still harvest all the wheat on this farm with those two. It would take a month, but you could do it."

In the far corner of the lot, two even older combines continue to undergo the gradual return to earth. Their tin carcasses
sag on iron struts, like hides on long-dead cattle. Beyond the
barbed wire, pasture stretches a half mile before coming to the
first field under a pivot sprinkler, which will water pinto beans
this year. "Serene" is the word that surfaces whenever I describe
this original prairie. A natural complement to the pale, yet very
blue, sky, the pastel green yearns in all directions, and the space
releases me. The sky and prairie—peaceful, orderly, quiet—take
no notice of me, confirming through indifference my ability to
accomplish anything I wish. This morning, my esteem-building
task was loading the horses. But things aren't working out so
well for Jake, whose grunting becomes audible to us as he
shoves the go-cart across the lot in our direction.

Yesterday, I recovered from the afternoon heat in Ron and
his wife Nila's air-conditioned double-wide trailer, and displayed, by local standards, my eccentricity as a parent. I
expressed reservations about letting Jake ride the go-cart. A
neighbor woman who had come over with her husband to visit
said, "Don't worry. The first three times they get on it, they're
careful. They go slow. About the fourth time, they go so fast you
just can't watch them anymore." The woman took a swig of her
iced tea. "You remember that, Jim? I just stayed in the house
and pulled the curtains."

Over the last couple days Ron and Nila have repeated this
sage advice. "Just can't watch 'em, that's all." In this culture,
mothers cast their male children to fate rather than endanger-
ing their manly futures with female worry. This censure of the
maternal often drove my mothers' hands to fist with tension
and caused her mouth to clamp down in silent worry. She's
been so schooled in keeping her emotions silenced that her
heart and concerns are inaccessible to me even now. Anything
Bruce writes about her, I know, cannot recognize the internal
knots a woman winds herself into here.

I ran after Jake for the first few minutes he was on the go-cart.

"Mother-henning him to death," would be the gist of local opinion. Bemused and chivalrous, Ron brought out the four-wheeler, the farm's latest acquisition, and in thirty seconds taught me how to drive it. I puttered after Jake, restarting the go-cart engine for him every time it stalled, until the mysterious carburetor refused completely. I secretly hoped Jake wouldn't get the engine going again this morning, and am glad to see him pushing the go-cart past us now, back toward the shop. "It keeps breaking down," he complains angrily—then, to impress Bruce, adds, "It's the carburetor."

"You'll have to resort to shooting sparrows with your B-B gun," Bruce says.

"Mom won't let me shoot birds."

"Oh Christ," Bruce says to me, "let him have a little fun."

My brother is a true Kansan. There's a tacit battle over authenticity between us, this in an age when everyone is questing for the real, and when, with better luck than either of us has had so far, you can sell your bona fide membership in a particular culture for a heady price in the literary marketplace. It's a battle I'm destined to lose because Kansas values are male. Parts of me simply can't have existence here.

I am happy to live in Laramie now, where these plains reach the mountains, but it was a long trek back to a place where I recognize the tone of the air, the pitch of the sky. Along the way, to my family's thinking, I picked up many harebrained notions. Sitting at the kitchen table in our parents' house in town yesterday, my brother and I listened as Dad told about a vicious feud a local farm family was having over land. All farmers' children fight on the demise of the patriarchs. Our parents fought with our aunts and uncles on both sides. Alluding to his and Mom's estate planning, Dad was sure there wouldn't be "any of that kind of squabbling around here."

No, I shook my head obediently, but I felt dimly unconvinced. Hadn't Bruce and I always squabbled?

Bruce said, "Julie can have all the buffalo grass, and I'll take the irrigated crop ground."

"And you just think I'm dumb enough to go for that, don't you?"

Bruce cackled. He raised his brows at me. "You can pasture your horses," he inveigled.

"And she won't have to kill any little animals or insects by farming," Dad said. "She's an en-viro-mentalist, you know."

It hurt, their teasing, the males with their heads on straight weighing in against me. They consider me an idiot when I suggest that the birds on the farm should be left alive or that the million gallons of water we pump daily in the summers will eventually drain the aquifer.

Dad shoved his chair back from the table and hobbled into the living room. I got him a cane for Christmas, which Mom says he uses, but I noticed it leaning in a corner of the kitchen, the label still attached.

He lowered himself into his easy chair, and stared down at his feet. "Look at those shoes," he said. They were reddish-brown Rockports, with rubber soles. "I bought those seven years ago, for that cruise." After our brother Clark's death, Dad had relented in his resistance to vacations and had taken Mom on a trip to the Caribbean. There's a picture on the mantel of the two of them on New Year's Eve—Dad with a plastic top hat perched ludicrously high on his bald head, Mom's face strained and wrinkled beneath her silvered, conical hat. Rubes in the Caribbean, their hearts aching for their lost son.

"I'll never need another pair of dress shoes," Dad said.

We are a family, united in loss and love, lacking the means to talk about either. So I try to let the political differences slide. The other day, after Jake cleaned up the dinner dishes for Mom, Dad said to him, "You'd make a good maid."

"Thank you," Jake said appreciatively, not catching the jibe. Though I said nothing, I seethed inside, remembering a conversation I had with Clark not too long before he died. We talked about how difficult it was when visiting Kansas to be the selves we'd evolved into elsewhere. He told me he once attempted, during a visit, to help Mom wash the dishes. Both she and Dad were appalled. The air grew so charged over that breach of tradition, he believed they suspected he was a closet homosexual.

While role rigidity prevents me from being my complete self at home, I also know that such limitations are what make this place this place. Culture, uniqueness, local flavor. Bias, narrowness, parochialism. These are reverse sides of the same coin. Native here, I am always trying to dispose of one side while keeping the other, an impossibility. Even a simple visit like this one, home to see my parents and pick up my horses, reignites my confusion. Staying to help my father farm—either with a husband, as he once expected me to do, or without one, as he allowed I just might be able to do when I returned after my second divorce—would have been a self-betrayal. But so was leaving.

The unquenchable thirst for the untrammeled and real drives the current interest in place-centered memoirs. I remember a famous *New Yorker* cover from the 1970s. In the foreground loomed Manhattan. Beyond the Hudson River, the rest of the country was a mild green patch with an abrupt mountain peak here and there, erroneously signifying Los Angeles, Texas, Las Vegas. Now the New York publishing industry is filling that map in, and my brother and I, fluent in Strunk and White, are vying to be the hired cartographers. It's hard to map a place when it's part of you, however. Or you're part of it. We are the map. We must flay ourselves and stretch our hides across glossy pages between perfume and vodka ads.

Sometimes I think I am a fool to aspire to that. Other times, I suspect that all people share the drive to be known in this way. Writing about our family and our farm will justify my father's love and quell his disappointment. The best we kids could do, in Dad's imagination, was carry on what Grandpa Ferd began. The only greater possibility Dad might recognize would be to depict him and his farm on the map of the world.

I suspect that my brother and I write for similar reasons. We write to portray the way allegiance to a father and a place complicates allegiance to the self. We write also because the impossible facts of recent experience—panicked phone calls from our mother and hours in the ICU in Denver, the nearest city with a good hospital—are beginning to convince us that our eighty-two-year-old father will die. Gradually, we're finding, the dust of middle age puts out the fires of youth, and from below the ash rises a foreboding monolith. We write because our father's veering skeleton and aging flesh still harbor light and love, and that light and love breathe up from the grass and rain down from the sky, alternately drying and wetting our skin. Dad is the sun generating the winds that blow in our fluted lungs and throats, giving us voice, this despite his own unpoetic emphasis on practicality.

"Now what you kids need to do," Dad says, for the millionth time, "is get out there and learn your way around. That farm is a good moneymaker, but it won't run itself." Sitting opposite him at the oval table, I'm impressed by his presence more than the familiar words. I'm baffled by how this passionate man, at the hub of my life despite the distance I've put between us over the years, can simply stop breathing. What will happen to all that drive, all that passion and will and volition?

He sits with his elbows on the table, his breakfast bowl shoved aside, hands folded. One hand strokes the back of the other, as if trying to figure out what happened to the huge strength that used to reside there, as if the hands are themselves remembering their lifetime of work, wondering at the absence of steel and tools beneath them. They are self-conscious hands now, having only each other to know and reckon with. His bald head tilts to the side—so much weight there, so much knowledge, so much life and interest still within him, despite his slowing heart. We kids long ago discovered that Dad had few material desires, except for farm tools, and those things he would provide for himself. So for years we've been giving him books on

Western history for Christmas and birthdays—Lewis and Clark's journals, various renditions of the battle at the Little Bighorn, homesteaders' diaries. He devours the books and recites them back to us, these histories of avarice and bloodshed underlying his own ordered and practical agriculture on the Plains.

His latest interest is outer space, but even popular books by Isaac Asimov and Carl Sagan are too hard for him now. "What with my brain like it is," he says. Because of this new dimension he's entering, I sense that he *needs* to understand space. Unlike Mom, he's never been religious, and so believes he'll only molder into the ground when he dies. But curiosity about what's beyond this planet, whose soil and sun he's known so intimately, eats away at him. "I always wanted to live until they found life in outer space," he says.

I get in the Rodeo, roll the window down, and stare up at Bruce. We know our dad is dying. Dad is dying. Bruce's book may make it to press in time, while it seems increasingly unlikely mine will. Meanwhile, we try on the art of conversation.

"Used to be," I complain to Bruce, "you couldn't write about places like this without being accused of regionalism. Now publishers can't seem to get enough of these backwaters."

Bruce takes a slow look around, appraising the metal Quonsets, the unoccupied two-story farmhouse with its flaking asbestos shingles, and the abandoned trailer houses and implements. The unromantic farmstead melds to a mile of bare ground to the north, where Dad keeps his summer fallow free of weeds so there will be enough moisture for the winter wheat when it's planted in September. "At least you don't have to worry about inducing an urban invasion. I don't think urbanites go in much for dirt."

I leaf mentally through the books I've read about places. Some of them eulogize. Some demythologize. I'm inclined to do both. I know that in writing about this place, I must first overcome the farm stereotype—the predictable boredom of silos, rolling hills, and plump, wholesome, shiny-faced families. Our land is treeless, flat, huge, and dry. In service of growing plant and animal life, Kansas farm people take on parched and sardonic countenances. They ruthlessly kill, with pesticides, harrows, guns, and technology, anything that comes between them and their single passion, harvest.

Living here means being blown and tossed by nature's whims. Rain, for instance, comes on its own terms. How it rains matters, and usually it doesn't rain right. The droplets strike the ground with the force of molten metal. Rain comes with hail, or high winds, or at the wrong time. Afterwards, the ground dries and hardens. Then blows. Huge dust clouds rise off the fields, and the farmers must work them fast to keep from losing crops and topsoil. Then comes a soft June morning like this one. The elements knead you from birth, until you are subject and receptive. Where you live becomes what you know, becomes who you are.

But knowledge that goes bone deep is the most difficult to convey, and the easiest to take for granted. I remember a camping trip in the Wyoming desert last summer with a New York friend. She was researching a book based on her experiences moving west. I felt I failed her when I didn't know the names of the wildflowers, or the history of the Union Pacific Railroad, or the geology of the region's mountains. I couldn't share with her the inspiration I drew from distance nor the way light and time fuse west of the hundredth meridian, entering people only through their immersion in both.

A breeze carries the scent of dame's rocket from near the barbed-wire pasture fence, where the farm foreman's wife, Nila, could, but doesn't, pick spring bouquets. Kansans have a narrow view of beauty. Outside their house yards, anything that isn't good for livestock forage is a weed. Yet the most complete version of myself lives here. Physical tasks like loading the horses confirm my skill outdoors with the products of the earth.

Now, if only I could convey my heart's knowledge in writing. If only I could cause this air to loft off the pages.

I want to write about Kansas in such a way that I transcend regionalism. My father wants life on other planets confirmed so that he won't be alone; somehow life beyond earth would make his death less final. For me, recognition and appreciation in New York of the life here would be almost as reassuring. All of the city's cultural arbiters, trapped as mortals in mortal families, are no less alone than we of sparser numbers on the less trodden and not always less sophisticated Plains.

"Want a ride up to the shop?" I ask Bruce.

He declines, but catches up to me as I'm replacing the bulb in the right taillight. Last November, in some quirk of forethought, I placed a spare bulb in the glove compartment. Proud of this well-timed display of preparedness, I remove the taillight glass by releasing the thick-gauged wire holding it in the fixture.

I wave Jake up from the sheep barn, where I see him headed with his B-B gun. He gets in, and we drive down to the double-wide. We meet Dad coming in from his morning constitutional, the current version being a drive around the cornfield in his air-conditioned Ford pickup. "Did you check the spare?" he asks out his window. I slap my forehead.

With Bruce standing awkwardly by, allowing me my independence, I open the trailer storage compartment, unload my saddle, roll out the tire and hoist it over Dad's tailgate. He drives me back to the shop, where I'm confronted with a new air compressor I don't know how to operate. He comes lumbering inside, lowers himself onto the back tire of a seed drill, and points to the lever closing off the hose. "Be sure to hang up the hose when you're done," he instructs. The job completed, I glimpse Dad's extended hand and realize he wants me to help him get up. I give a brief yank to which his body doesn't respond. Then, sobered by his genuine weakness, I carefully support his elbow with one hand and pull him up with the other. He rises creakily to a stoop, and I savor his grip. He knows

I do this, and I think he does it too. Any touch now might be our last. I look around me, recording the ambiance inside the dark shop, with its scent of tractor grease, Malathion, dust, and cow dung, then follow him outside and catch a ride the fifty yards back to my car.

Now I'm standing outside Dad's pickup in front of the house he first lived in with my mother before they moved onto her parents' place. In his life, he's seen farming go from horses to mega-tractors almost as big as this house, but he's always toiled under the same sun. He's always looked out on the same plain, with the same knobs and rills. Behind me awaits the rig with which I'll make my perennial exit.

"What do you think of my hat?" Dad asks. Bright white and embroidered with the name of an implement dealer, it's impossibly high and round. The flat brim lends no dash to eyes that have not, at least, lost their power to insinuate.

"It makes you look really sexy." He preens, cocking his head and baring his teeth in an exaggerated smile. He is a shell. We both know that. His grin is an old man's—lots of gold, the bottom teeth yellowed, worn, and angled inward. I grip his shoulder. Instead of the blue shirts he's worn on the farm forever, this morning he dressed in the same bright orange one he wore to supper last night at the Buckboard. The owner, once a classmate of Bruce's, came over and joked with Dad about his lack of appetite. "That's not all I've lost," Dad said. Mom and the owner's laughs were more exaggerated than the allusion would have elicited in the past. Across our plates of half-eaten hot beef sandwiches, Bruce and I exchanged looks recognizing this.

The town-shirt worn in daylight on the farm conveys resignation. Feeling the bones beneath it, I realize I'm gripping Dad the way he used to grip me. He would squeeze and release as he did Mom's dinner rolls, looking for the one done to perfection. "Stay offa that tractor now," I say.

"I will if you kids come out here and keep me off it."

I've already told him I plan to help sow wheat in

September, and Bruce has made the trip out from Schoenchen a dozen times in the last two years. Bruce has helped out a lot, Dad says. But fact is, we're one generation beyond the farm. My city friends who work in computers call themselves "information processors" and "data pushers." Like them, even when our writing earns the badge of art, Bruce and I deal in ephemeral words, a product no one can touch, taste, or smell. The term "lived experience," which appears in the composition texts I sometimes teach from, has always seemed redundant to me, but it speaks volumes about our times. The lives my brother and I once had, in the dirt of the farm yard and in the fields beyond, are memories.

Over the last few years, our father has dwelled increasingly in the realm of memory. After he recovered from a stroke and began driving out to the farm again in his pickup, he heard ragtime piano music as vividly as if the piano were in the cab with him. He'd never been a musician, yet somewhere in his mind the notes had stored themselves in perfect order. He would pull his pickup onto the shoulder and tap out the beat on his steering wheel, until a passing neighbor would stop and inquire if he needed help.

After the stroke, he also recalled Grandpa Bair advising him not to expand his farm beyond what he could handle. "Don't try to get too big," his father warned him. Dad says it seemed as if old Ferd were standing before him, in his overalls and bright yellow plaid shirt. "You're not made like that. It would drive you crazy." This advice must have sunk in when it was originally given, for Dad declined to buy more wheat ground in the seventies, when land went up to a thousand an acre. And he didn't lose his farm, as so many neighbors did when crop prices fell and they were unable to pay their mortgages.

Another vivid, almost supernatural memory returns to him from childhood, when he attended school in the neighboring town of St. Francis. He remembers a pale little girl with long, dark hair standing by his desk, waiting. She doesn't say a thing, only holds out a pencil. Finally, he figures out to say, "Do you want me to sharpen your pencil?" and she nods. He sharpens it with his pocketknife. "Gosh," he puzzles, repeating the scene at the kitchen table, "didn't we have pencil sharpeners back then?"

"Well, I know we did," says Mom, who went to grade school in the country and high school in Goodland.

"We must not have. That little girl wasn't there by the end of the year. She got to coughing up blood, grew sicker and sicker, died finally. The Eggers didn't have any money and they didn't take her to the doctor or to the hospital. They were some crazy religion, you know, and the girl's mother, talking to my mom about it, said, 'His will be done.' Well, my Gawd...." Dad's voice trails off.

He can't get that little girl out of his mind. Neither can I. She waits, not speaking.

At Forty-five

At seven in the morning, dressed for work, I grab the chicken out of the refrigerator, where it's been thawing overnight. I've stored it on a plate, thereby avoiding a drying, sticky blood pool on the lower shelf and drips across the linoleum. I remembered the plate because I'm at that eternal middle-age of my mother in all my childhood memories. That responsible age when experience has taught us the consequences of carelessness.

I shout through the dining room and up the stairs to my son, "Jake, get up! You've got only half an hour before the bus comes!" At the sink, I cut the plastic wrapper away from the chicken, rinse out the body cavity, clean it as best I know how, toss it into the Crock-Pot, and sprinkle it with salt and pepper.

My mother raised her own chickens. Placed a stick across their necks, stood on both ends, and pulled. They danced headless among their peers, blood spurting until they wound down and collapsed. Mom would pick them up before their legs stopped churning. Outside, on the porch stoop, we would grasp their scrawny legs as if they were the stems of some vegetable we'd harvested and dip the bodies into a kettle of water Mom had boiled over the gas range. We would pluck their feathers, a tedious, stinky job. Then my mother would take her position at the kitchen sink, where she would expertly wield her favorite paring knife, the one she'd sharpened so many times that the blade was only a quarter inch wide.

Sometimes my father would stroll through the kitchen, in from washing off field dirt on the mud porch, his sun-blackened, hairy arms dripping water. Spotting her rear, which must have seemed an irresistible target beneath the gathers of her housedress, he would mischievously swat it.

"Ooh!" she'd yell as if angry. "Har-old!"

He would say things that I didn't know I needed to forgive him for then, but which I do, without much effort, now. Such as, "What's the matter? I'm just inspecting my property."

Her fried chicken was the best, crusty and amber, never doughy or greasy. I always chose the wishbone, which Mom cut as a separate piece. I didn't know then that her style of parceling chickens was not universal. I just know now, when I stand at my sink in the big house I bought because it reminds me of the big house I grew up in, that my hands look like my mother's against the painfully naked chicken. Our hands—hers then, mine now—are bony and veined, and beneath our long fingers, the chicken's wet skin is the same color as our own. The knobby bone ends look the way our knuckles would look, were our knives to slip. When I rub my hands, which are beginning to suffer from arthritis, they remind me of the slick, cool way my mother's hands felt in all those thousands of purposeful and inadvertent touches between mother and child. The hands say "age" to me, age and love and soil and mortality. Soil, because we drew our lives from it; and Mom nurtured beauty by way of it, in her immense flower garden. She would stand up while hoeing and splay her hands alternately, working the fingers back and forth. Dad used to make jokes about Mom sleeping with Arthur Itis.

My mother would have called herself a housewife, although there was never an occasion for anyone to ask. Everyone knew that she was just one of John and Lizzie Carlson's daughters, who had married Harold, one of the Bairs. They lived on the farm her parents had built through the typical fifty years of familial perseverance. Jasmin and Harold had three children, two boys and me.

She never taught me, I never learned, how to cut up a chicken. She assumed that I would absorb this knowledge from observing her and that when my day came to stand at the sink, I would wield my own knife as expertly as she. On my visits home, I've never had the courage to admit my ignorance, my reluctance intensifying as the years advance. How could I be forty-five, my mother's age when fried chicken dinners were common fare summer noons, and not be practiced in this essential art?

My mother taught me even less about romance than she taught me about chickens. She assumed I would absorb this knowledge also and slip into a marriage similar to hers. Because our lives were so interwoven by timeless sun, land, and air, they too seemed timeless, deceptively static. Life on land deluded us into believing in the generations. Each season the kingbirds returned to the locust tree in Mom's south yard. Each year they sent out fledglings who returned the following year with mates and built nests in the nearby box elders. My mother thought some neighbor boy would find me, the way Harold had found her. We would nest on land not far down the road. She expected one of her children to take up residence on the home place, farming the same ground, drawing sustenance from the same vegetable garden and from the descendants of the same livestock, forever.

We lived under the illusion we *had* gone on forever. But in fact, my family had not been on Kansas soil long. Mom's Scandinavian parents crossed the Atlantic on separate boats. They met in Iowa, where their families first settled, then made the trek to Kansas on their own. My father's grandparents migrated from Pennsylvania to Nebraska. His parents also came to Kansas as adults. These two adventurous couples produced seven children each. Mom and Dad, born during this swell of productivity, on land and at the hearth, were unaware of their parents' pasts elsewhere. They couldn't foresee the influences that would reach out to their children, through the schools and over the airwaves, and pull the tide back. Today, they are the living, beached remnants of our family, whose skeletons lay strewn across the Kansas plain like fossils swept inland by a tidal wave.

The sixties reached in and got me. They were presaged by James Dean movies played over our family's black and white TV. Nothing excited me more than imagining the love of such a wounded, troubled boy. He might be a rebel without a cause, but, for the lucky girl who got him, a cause in and of himself.

By the time I graduated from high school, there were causes aplenty. I rode the tidal wave out of Kansas in the boat of the older, renegade son of a wealthy Milwaukee, Wisconsin manufacturing family. His parents didn't understand him. They understood him so poorly in fact that they had committed him to Menninger's, the famous mental institution in Topeka, on the opposite end of the state from Goodland. He really wasn't very crazy, only misaligned, which appealed to me in the beginning. Our conveyance was his '56 silver T-Bird convertible, which he drove into town in May 1967, the month I turned eighteen. He came to hunt pheasants, and a mutual friend arranged a blind date between us. I attended a semester of college at KU, in the eastern part of the state near Topeka, where he continued to live, then we motored out of Goodland in January of 1968, trailing tin cans.

My parents consented to the marriage, they say today, because they had no choice. I was headstrong and would have done what I wanted anyway. But I think I could have benefited from a little maternal instruction in the ways of the heart.

My mother skirts the personal topics—death, religion, love. If I say something provocative, she says only "Well ..." in the manner of all the women of my childhood. Then nothing. I've learned not to wait for the insights which I suspect would follow, if only it were okay to express emotion. Her deeper feelings are mostly inaccessible to me. If she had told me what it was like being my father's wife, what she felt when she first met him, how those feelings changed as their marriage matured, then perhaps I wouldn't have been so handicapped by the

absence of intimate knowledge of the people I was supposed to
know most intimately. In fairness, she had no training in such
talk and didn't know I would need it. In the wave came, out I
went. Nothing had prepared her for the need to instruct her
daughter in the obvious.

I've had this image in my mind ever so long
now. Her hands, mine, as naked as the chicken. My mother, me,
at the kitchen sink, preparing a meal for our family. She still pre-
pares many chickens, although she doesn't fry them. "It's the
cholesterol," she says. "I have to be careful of Harold's heart."
Often when I've visited in the last few years, I've heard her
complain, while standing at her aqua sink, "These store-
boughten chickens are just terrible anymore."

"Terrible?" I once asked.

"Yes."

"How? Terrible?"

"It's all this godawful crap you have to scrape out of them,
and the fat. Chickens never used to be like that."

She told me about a younger neighbor woman who, when
Mom mentioned cleaning a hen for supper, said, "Clean what?
I just stick 'em in the oven."

"Can you imagine that?" my mother asked me.

I shook my head in supposed equal disgust.

Since then I've raked my fingers over the interiors of chickens while running warm water inside, ripping loose the remnants of kidneys and other gutty things. I've trimmed the
chunks of fat that hang loose near the tail. I've done this doubt-
fully, without much hope that I'll ever understand what a truly
cleaned chicken is supposed to look like. Yet I am becoming my
mother in the way that we all do—feeling her body aches, her
bafflement at the passage of years, the growth of children, fore-
seeing minor household catastrophes and taking precautions
(the plate under the chicken and a dozen other preventive
measures daily). I see these similarities for the first full, real

time, living in this house reminiscent of the farmhouse, at this
alarming age.

      The differences are these. I have a job outside
the house, no husband, and only one son. I am not rearing him
on the farm where I grew up. The boy I attempt to rouse with
shouts as I stuff the chicken into the Crock-Pot is the son of a
cowboy I met and married after rejecting the city life that beckoned so beguilingly when I was eighteen. I thought I had
learned much in that first marriage about what not to do, much
on how not to choose. But I had yet to overcome my penchant
for misunderstood men. The image my second husband pat-
terned himself after reached us both in childhood. In Kansas, it
came in with the sixties also, over the airwaves and out of my
family's blond-cabineted, splay-legged Zenith TV, packaged in
what my mother told me were "psychological" westerns. To her
credit, she complained about these, preferring the old
Hopalong Cassidy days when it was easy to sort the good guys
from the bad. Bad guys having reasons for their badness seemed
like excusing them to her, and she worried about the influence.
I couldn't see what bothered her so much. Having compassion
for the makings of an individual seemed only Christian.

    Now I understand she was troubled by the attractiveness of
that new breed of bad men. The injustices in their pasts made
them appealing martyrs. She had every right to worry. My first
sex fantasy involved one of those psychologically wounded
cowboy types. He was Roy Rogers, complete with the red shirt,
except angry, gone awry. Roy Rogers injured by A Past. We
became hopelessly entwined. I helped him return to the right
side of the law, but he was always in danger of backsliding, and
the evil in him could be appeased only with sex. He needed my
body. My sex shifted in these fantasies. One time I would be the
girl in the leather fringe skirt. Other times I was the traumatized
Roy. It was more fun being Roy, with all his license for evil born
of the harm society had done him. That wasn't an option in

reality, of course. I was wired for Dwayne.

We met when I was living in a remote region of the Mojave Desert, attempting to teach myself two things—how to write and how to be alone in the world, because that's how I found myself after my divorce. He worked as a cowboy on the OX Ranch, run by a couple who also owned the little cabin I was refurbishing to live in. He was handsome, charming, sexy, and had a criminal past. But he was bad for reasons—reasons I could sympathize with.

Like me, he wore the rebellious assumptions of our generation on his face, in his gestures. When I left San Francisco, I had told my friends, jokingly, that I was searching for a Buddhist cowboy. He wasn't that, but he did seem a remarkable mixture—a cowboy with a mind for something other than horses, dogs, and doggies. He played chess, read pretty good books for pleasure. He was also a Vietnam vet, and our chemistry had something to do with our mutual alienation.

Like me, he had gotten himself to the Mojave, where Joshua trees, juniper, piñon pine, and shoulder-high prickly pear dappled the cordillera mountain ranges. He viewed the desert with as much awe as I did. With as much hope. He was the essence of potential, hampered until then by circumstances. Potential on the remake. "You're my lifeboat," he said. He quit drinking, but started again within a few months of our wedding. When drunk or disappointed, he became abusive, which should have been no surprise. We separated after only eight months of marriage, when I was two months pregnant.

In this case, I'd had the option of listening to my mother, although she never made her advice explicit. She disliked the psychological westerns, but liked Dwayne, probably because she didn't know the full extent of his past. Had she known he had robbed a bank and spent two years in prison before coming to the Mojave, she may have said a word or two.

A glance at the clock on the coffee machine confirms what I feared. It is getting late. I jog up the stairs, trying to ignore the pain in my knee, and, sure enough, find Jake's door still closed. I knock. "Jake! Time to get up." I enter the room and discover that, once again, he slept with the TV on. I allow him a TV in his room only for playing Nintendo games. The reception is so poor that, without cable, he gets mostly snow, but I've caught him late at night sitting up staring at it with the volume low. He's able to detect the ghostly images of cops beating black boys into submission on real life police dramas and women being stalked by serial killers. It's a vicious cycle, the TV painting the fears behind his eyes and simultaneously dispelling them with a light he thinks is soothing, but which I find eerie and alienating, even immoral. "That's disgusting," I tell him often, hearing my mother's tone in my voice. "Making entertainment of other people's suffering."

"Oh Mom," Jake says. "It's just TV."

"Nothing's just TV."

I pick up his heavy, ridiculously wide-legged jeans and shake them out. "I guess you can wear these again. They're not too dirty." I know I'll have a fight on my hands if I require him to wear his Levis instead of the oversized designer jeans he saved up his allowances to buy. He identifies with the delinquents, not the police. Given that limited choice, I would too. He's a very good boy, compassionate, funny, sensitive, but I worry about the influences just the same.

Jake says, "Oh Mom. Why don't you just let me sleep in today?"

"Can't, kiddo. Up now. It's time for breakfast." I'll break the news to him over Cheerios. No more TV nightlight, and no more TV in his room if he uses it for anything other than games. Tonight, over chicken, I'll ask him about school. After supper, I'll look at his art work and his writing and I'll state what should be obvious. I'll tell him he's talented and smart, that I believe in his abilities. As he grows older, I'll begin telling him more. That he doesn't need a girl to love him in order to prove himself valid. I'll tell him not to rush into marriage. It is better to wait and find the right person than to compromise his heart.

When he is a teenager, I'll tell him this. When you choose a mate, choose her not just for beauty or sex appeal. Choose her for character. You'll want a woman you can talk to about everything, who observes her own and others' hearts. You will want to stay with her, so choose very carefully. Because it hurts to leave someone you don't love enough just as much as it hurts when someone you love very much leaves you.

I will have to admit, as I'm conveying all this, that I didn't heed my own advice. Not having the benefit of such instruction from my mother is only partly why I screwed up. She and Dad gave me a good childhood and I could have chosen to follow her example, even if not in all details. Instead, I rebelled, turning my back on my parents' life when I was eighteen. By the time I reached thirty, those details had gained in appeal. I began to picture the life I'd opted out of, down the road from my parents in a big farmhouse of my own, cows and sheep in the lot by the barn.

I've wished I could stand at a sink with a window over it, my hands extending down through a chicken's guts into the earth of a flower garden. I would look out that window and see my parents' place. My son would marry eventually and move there. A few miles west, and some other relatives would be living in Grandpa Bair's old place. This is the way it was supposed to work out.

"Grandpa Bair's," we say, not "Grandma and Grandpa Bair's." This is partly why it didn't. Like my grandmothers, my mother submitted to her husband's rule of the household. He was a benevolent dictator whose dominion no one thought to question. I could not have married a man from down the road because he would have wanted to rule as my father did. I would have wanted to share decisions in the shop and field as well as in the house. That's the kind of daughter my parents somehow raised.

But I will acknowledge this to Jake—I didn't have to marry someone down the road or become a housewife in order to choose a better man, someone of his grandfather's mettle. My child is fatherless at least partly as a consequence of my own carelessness.

I'll tell him other things as well. *Land and where you are from are part of who you are.* That's why I moved us to Laramie, where there are mountains and undestroyed wilderness for him to fall in love with. He may want to leave when he grows up, but then he'll want to come back. I will tell him all this often, the obvious.

Wheat Harvest, 1997

We drive out there in Dad's pickup, my son Jake and I. To the neighbors along the gravel road, we must look like an apparition. *There goes Harold,* they've been saying for over sixty years, the brief comment conveying amusement, envy, and respect.

We're harvesting Dad's last wheat crop, the one he planted but will not reap. A month ago, in his hospital bed, he wondered aloud whether he should trade this pickup in. "I usually trade every two years," he announced to me, my mother, and her minister, who had dropped by on his regular rounds.

I liked Pastor Dan, as my mother called him. He had been supportive of her when Dad was sick in the past, but I found his ministerial air off-putting that morning. There Dad was, attempting to play the host from his prone and diminished position, and there the minister was, standing two heads taller than I, towering over Mom, who, wearing a perpetual look of worried boredom, sat in the plastic molded chair at the foot of the bed. He made the room small, and I knew he thought we were in denial, a trendy, simple analysis. He didn't understand my family's unwillingness to comfort each other with notions of a hereafter in which only Mom believed. He was raised in Minnesota, a country of small farms and unquestioning Christianity. It was inconceivable to him that my father, a "man of the soil," could be an unbeliever. Mom had been a Lutheran since childhood, though, and Pastor Dan was determined to say a prayer over the heathen. He bided his time as Dad bragged about a book my brother had recently published, complained about the recent drought, praised the mettle of his farm foreman Ron, and fretted that trading the pickup might be a waste of money. "I don't hardly get enough use out of it anymore," he said. "It just sits in the garage most of the time."

Traditionally, Dad bought basic models, but, announcing that by God he'd earned it, he decided this pickup would have it all. It's a Ford F-250 four-wheel-drive, with air-conditioning, electric windows, and a stereo cassette player. There are kernels scattered about on the bench seat and in the truck bed—pink, chemically treated seed corn, and smatterings of wheat and pinto beans. And on the floor between Jake and me rest a flannel-lined denim jacket and a pair of overshoes, still caked with dried mud. These items are too suggestively inert.

Someone, probably my niece or nephew, gave Dad a zippered leather cassette carrier for Christmas, and it still sits on the dash unopened, the cardboard wrapper gritty with dust. I doubt Dad ever plugged a cassette into a truck or tractor stereo in his life. I don't think he ever switched on this radio. He kept his mind busy computing. Farmers have calculators built into their heads on which they are forever multiplying acreage times yields times dollars and cents per bushel or per hundred weight, then subtracting costs of fertilizer, diesel fuel, herbicides, labor, and tare factors.

I don't even know what the tare factor is on wheat—how much we'll be docked if there's chaff in with the grain or if the moisture content is too high. I don't know what too high is. So it's ironic that I'm driving Dad's truck, looking, to the neighbors who live a mile or so off the road, like a resurrection of Harold. It is a false testament to continuance. I did a stint back on the farm when Jake was a baby, but I "just didn't have the head for farming," Dad conceded, when I told him I was going back to college. Driving tractors over these barren-looking, but in fact quite fertile fields, I shouted story ideas into a miniature tape recorder, which, whenever Dad was around, I kept concealed in my jacket pocket. Invariably, engaged in writing fictions, I would fail to attend to fact and screw something up. I would take a sharp turn when pulling the disks, forgetting that you could do that to the left but not to the right, and would pile the hitch up on the tractor tire.

It's not that you can't think and do fieldwork at the same time, it's just that farming is a jealous god requiring obedience to its own concerns. Dad would calculate implement widths times miles, reduce the product to square rods and extrapolate to acres. Factoring in tractor speed, he would compute exactly how long it would take him and the rest of his "men"—Ron, Ron's wife Nila, and I—to finish our fields. He would envision his move to the next field, deciding who would lose the least time by following him over in his pickup. The aim was to keep the tractors moving.

I left these calculations to my father and tried to do what I considered my own real work. Sometimes I was so oblivious that I would fail to see him waiting in his pickup at the end of the field. I would lift the implement out of the furrows, make my turn, jam the hydraulic lever forward, and push the throttle back against its stop, applauding myself on how handy I'd gotten with the turn brake. I would be shouting into my tape recorder again when I'd see his pickup racing past me on the nearest road, his lights flashing, his arm straight out the window, his hand flat as he made a lowering motion. I would look over my shoulder and discover that a hydraulic hose had broken and the disk or drill or cultivator—whatever I was pulling—had failed to go back in the ground.

"I couldn't figure out what the hell you were doing," I once told him. "Sieging Heil?"

"I was trying to tell you to pay a little goddamned attention."

"Can I drive?" Jake asks.

I pull over and put the gearshift in park. Jake slides across while I go around. Jake is twelve this year, but most farmers let their kids drive pickups when they are much younger—at seven

or eight. As a consequence, every year local papers report overturned trucks, smashed children. But I do regret Jake's not having grown up on a farm. There's little division between work and
home life, and kids naturally learn responsibility at a young age.
The Meidingers' kids, for instance, work alongside their parents.

Ken and Susan Meidinger and their crew have been cutting
our wheat for the last eight years. They live in North Dakota, but
trailer all their machinery down to the Texas Panhandle each
summer, then work their way north, cutting for a regular and
satisfied clientele. We've come to count on them the way
Capistranoans await the return of swallows. Wheat is so plentiful in Kansas that all the tasks attendant on it seem like natural
patterns—migrations or flowerings. Today the fields are blooming with combines, and too late, I remember that the roads are
likely to be sprouting trucks. We didn't encounter any on the
way out, probably because the wheat's moisture content was
still too high earlier. But now the combines are moving and
here comes one of the Meidinger drivers, hauling the day's first
load. To Goodland or to Ruleton? Has anyone considered the
comparative solvency of the elevator companies? Which would
we rather have a contract with? This is just one of the thousands
of decisions Dad made every year.

"Slow down and pull over," I tell Jake.

He steps on the brake and the pickup skids to a stop in the
middle of the road. I have to stay calm and remember that the
Meidinger drivers know, from habit, to watch out for Harold's
pickup. He tended to wander the road, gazing at fields.

"Mom! What do I do?" Jake is starting to panic.

"Take your foot off the brake, but don't give it any gas. Let
it idle forward," I instruct him, trying to convey confidence.
"Okay, steer over to the side of the road. Not too far. That's it,
now stop and let it go by."

Susan Meidinger waves a tan, hefty arm and flashes a white
smile. Dust explodes all around us, road gravel spattering steel.
Too late, I shout, "Roll up your window!"

Jake jabs the electric controls in his armrest, locking and unlocking the doors. Finally, he manages to get his window rolled up. He leans back in his seat and says "Phew!" Forgetting that the truck is already running, he turns the switch, grinding the starter, revs the engine, then reaches up and puts the transmission in Drive. We peel out. Soon, feeling like a master of the road again, he says, "I'm doing just fine, aren't I?"

"Yes, you're doing great." I curl my toes in my boots and press the floorboard with both feet.

By the time we finally bump out into the field opposite the section where they're cutting, Jake is convinced he's ready for a solo mission. "Do you wanna just wait here while I go find Ron?" he asks.

Across the road to the south, dust billows behind a tractor in one of the irrigated circles. "Ron's busy in the pintos. If we needed to talk to him we'd drive over there. But we don't. Okay?"

"All right, but if you want to go somewhere, just ask me."

We call the field they're cutting simply "the section," six hundred forty acres. We wait behind one of the Meidingers' big trucks, our engine idling. I am like my father in this, running the air-conditioner with the windows open. It used to drive Mom crazy, but Dad couldn't stand being deprived of fresh air. A combine comes to the end of the field, raises its platform and veers toward us over the dirt.

Quicker on the trigger now, Jake closes the windows against the approaching dust. We watch the wheat pour out of the John Deere's green auger, some of the grain bouncing off the truck tarp and raining down on the hood of the pickup. When his bin is empty, Ken Meidinger turns the auger and combine engines off and climbs down from the cab.

I step into the wheat-curing heat of July. When I last worked here, the summer Jake was five, I took pride in being able to stand up under the heat as I toted irrigation socks on my shoulder, changing the settings on the quarter-mile stretches of pipe.

Since then, Dad converted to sprinkler irrigation, which is a lot less labor intensive. The section is dryland, though. I walk over to meet Ken.

He is a short, slight man and wears glasses. Were it not for his sun-darkened skin and calloused hands he might easily be mistaken for an accountant. But Kenny's a firecracker, Dad always said, and I know that he takes his own farming, up in North Dakota, and his custom cutting business too seriously. He worries and micromanages, as Dad always did. He's only forty, but suffers from high blood pressure.

Once, when Dad and I were having our lunch bucket dinners in Kenny and Susan's trailer, which they haul behind their pickup and park at our farm, we watched as Susan dumped Kenny's pills onto his plate. Seeing this caused Dad to worry. Who would we get to cut if Kenny "up and had a heart attack?" He felt the same about Ron, and that was one of the things he told Pastor Dan the day before he died. "There's a firecracker, for you," Dad said, his own voice hollow with age and tiredness, his bald head and barrel chest propped erect so that the fluid in his lungs would bother him less. "I don't know what we'd do without him." Everything he said in those last hours seemed to assume that "we" would go on forever.

"How's it doin'?" I ask Ken. I suspect that Kenny is thinking the same thing I am. The proceeds from the sale of my father's last crop will go at least partially into my bank account. We each know I've done little to earn this windfall other than love my father, and, despite Dad's flaws, that was never hard to do.

"Land almighty, Julie," Kenny says. "Apparently you don't need rain to grow wheat in Kansas." I hear the familiar North Dakota accent, Ken's German forebears still putting their lilt in his vowels and honing his T's to fine points. He's referring to the scant moisture we've had this year. "Or Harold didn't need rain anyway," Kenny adds.

"Why? What's it makin'?"

"My computer says it's averaging forty-three." Kenny smiles

widely and nods. He is a modern farmer. A control panel in each of his combines displays up-to-the-second data, the yields varying constantly by tenths of a percent, and he carries a pocket calculator. But even if he externalizes his math, he still shares the obsession. Like my father, he is perennially computing the bottom line. I'm wondering what that will be for him this year. *Twelve, twelve, and twelve,* Dad always said, citing the formula for paying custom cutters, but I'm no longer sure what the three twelves refer to.

Kenny's eyes move onto Jake, who is just now getting out of the truck. Is Kenny thinking what I suspect he is? That a farm boy would have done that instantly?

Jake lifts a hand, smiles, crosses the distance between us. When he comes up beside me, I can see Kenny noting his height. Jake's almost as tall as I am this year. "So you're driving Grandpa Harold's truck now?" Kenny says. "Won't be long and you'll be taking over."

"Uh." Jake looks around at the many fields. "Okay," he says. It's hard to see the humorous expression of doubt in his eyes, because of the severe curve he's worked into the bill of his black cap. Even though the flag stitched onto it and the inner band are gray with dirt, I can't convince Jake to part with the hat. He chose it purposefully to confuse people who might otherwise typecast him according to his wide-legged pants and rap group T-shirt.

"Oh come on." Kenny lightly punches Jake in the upper arm. Dad used to drop a hand onto Jake's shoulder and squeeze, waiting for him to duck out of his grip. "You're next in line, unless your Mom's going to run it?"

I smile, tilt my head, shrug. It's shameful, I know. I want the income from the farm, but don't want to sacrifice my own interests for it.

"And your uncle Bruce is too busy writing books," Kenny continues. His eyes land on Jake's flag while his lips set themselves in a steady line.

"My mom's a writer too, you know," Jake says. My son's compassion often amazes me. He knows I'm envious of Bruce's book. Jake adds, "She's got a book getting sold right now."

"Is that right?" Kenny says, generously impressed.

"Well that's what I'm hoping. There are no guarantees. Writing's kind of like farming that way."

Kenny laughs politely, but I know he's anxious to get back to work.

"Anyway," I tell him, "thanks for stopping. We'll just hope we inherited Old Harold's luck." I like calling my dad "Old Harold." It makes me feel as if I've stepped into his unfillable shoes. He called his father "Old Ferd."

Kenny extends his hand, and when I give him mine, he grasps and pats it. His cap bill lowers as his green eyes, enlarged by thick lenses, focus directly on mine. "You just let us know if there's anything we can do."

I look toward the field where all three of the Meidingers' combines edge along the wheat like robotic dinosaurs. "You're doing it," I say. "You're already doing it all." He lets my hand go.

"Do you think you could give Jake a ride? I wanted him to kind of get a feel for it, you know."

"Sure." Ken winks at Jake. "I'll get Jessica to take him."

"Jessica!" Jake complains, his voice low as we walk back to the pickup.

He shuts his door, on the passenger side now, a little harder than called for. "God, Mom. A *ride* in a combine? A *ride*? I thought I was going to drive one."

We sit and watch the dinosaurs nibble around the edge of the field. Pretty soon one of them reaches the near corner and turns toward us. We can see the thin, tall, tow-headed Jessica through the floor-to-ceiling cab glass. "I don't know," Jake says. "This is pretty embarrassing."

"Go on, it'll be fun."

"What do I do, sit in her lap?"

Jake tries to suppress his smile. "Oh, all right. Here goes."

He gets out and trots across the stubble, his pant legs flapping like loose awnings. He climbs the ladder of the idling combine in a few strides, but ducks, almost losing his grip on the rail when Jessica reaches over and throws open the door. She pulls the jump seat down for him, and Jake waves from inside the cab, already content. The boss's grandson and the custom cutter's daughter. If the boss were here he would say, "You may as well go back to town. You won't be seeing him for awhile. That Jessica's quite a looker."

"So's Jake," I would point out, always eager to apply my father's discriminatory standards equally to males.

He would nod, oblivious. "He's an awfully nice-acting boy." Nice-acting for boys, nice-looking for girls.

The combine bounces back into the field, the spreader fan on the tail end spewing. I switch on the wipers and beat the dust and chaff from the windshield, then turn off the engine and get out. The combines are far enough away that I can barely hear them, and the quiet that descends is the same quiet I've always known here. It makes my own existence seem surreal, uncertain. The horizon is round, flat, farmed. It's the type of landscape in which you must always have a passion, a purpose. Otherwise you dissipate, lose track of yourself, lapse into sorrow.

The sun presses against my back as I cross the dirt of this other section. This will be next year's wheat, so the ground is fallow for now. I dig with my toe the way I've seen Dad—Old Harold—do a thousand times. I've always taken this dirt for granted, but I learned reading my brother's book that it is loess, a fertile, wind-deposited silt-loam that nourishes wheat to perfection. Today I remove four or five inches before the dry gray gives way to moist brown. We need rain before we plant in September. We need it. I'm uncertain what we should do if none comes. Plant shallow and hope for a cloudburst? I thumb through the mostly vacant files in my stunted internal computer. Dad probably would have rodded instead of disking the weeds. The rod doesn't go in as deep and doesn't dry the soil

out as much. Then he would have gone over it all with the pack-
er, compressing the dirt so the surface was closer to moisture.
But I know Ron always disagreed with Dad about packing, and
when I mentioned the possibility to my brother the other day,
he said it wasn't good for the ground. Compressed it too much.
Are we to start doing things differently for the first time in sixty
years? I can picture the sparse stand come October. Dad would
say something disparaging: *No thicker than grass on a gnat's ass.*

The diesel truck engine starts up. Realizing I've broken a
cardinal farm rule by parking behind another vehicle, I scurry
over to the pickup and move it out of the way. I get out and
squat in the small square of shade cast by the cab. I watch the
combines. Time is normally a river, but here in this Kansas summer, the flow stalls in the heat. It's as if no time at all has passed
since my childhood. Each July, the wheat bends before the sick-
les. This has been happening for so long that the wheat's return
does seem like an independent act of nature, like wind or the
return of summer itself, not a logical response to some man's
labor, some man's will.

From the end of the dirt trail leading out of the field, I can
hear the truck's engine wind tighter as its driver shifts down.
Driving truck was my harvest job during the summers I lived
here, just after Jake was born and during those few years I came
back for the season. Dad was still ramrodding his harvests then,
still cutting some of the wheat himself and hauling as much as
he could to town in our own trucks in order to save on harvest
costs. (That was one of the twelves! Twelve cents for every
bushel hauled.) After my truck was loaded and tarped, Dad
would thump the door. "Take 'er to town," he would say, and I
would depress the clutch with my toe and lurch out of the field
in the lowest gear. Granny low, Dad called it. I was the only person who ever took the trucks up through all the gears. Most
drivers started in what I would call second.

I didn't barrel down the road, as Dad complained Ron did,
but drove carefully, slowing way down before the turns. The

bed tilted even when I took them wide. My own importance seemed magnified beneath the weight of the load. I hadn't been allowed to help with fieldwork as a girl, so I relished the task as an adult. Going to town with a load on, I had felt like a privileged acolyte. I was performing a ritual task, hauling one truckful, one ten-thousandth, maybe, of one Kansas county's wheat. I had no choice but to sacrifice sleep and to work hard. The wheat itself seemed to be making a sacrifice in turn.

I hadn't the wherewithal to teach my son through long practice, but hoped that, riding in the combine, he would look down and be transfixed as I had been as a child by the spectacle of millions of stalks submitting to the scythe. Heads laden, they fell beneath the reel, were amputated by the cutterbar, then crushed by the header's spiraling steel auger and guided into the bowels of the combine. The magnitude would inhabit his spirit, I hoped, as it had mine.

Back in that hospital room, in May, Pastor Dan finally got his deed accomplished. "Would it be all right if I said a prayer, Harold?"

"Well yes," Dad said, "I suppose that would be okay." I have never been able to sit, or in this case, stand, through a prayer without taking peaks around me. It is some odd, specialized attention deficit I suffer from. Dad kept his hands folded on his chest where they'd been lying all morning and, for the first time ever during a prayer, closed his eyes. I was embarrassed for him, on display in his hospital bed, and a little irritated with Pastor Dan's presumptuousness. He was taking advantage of my unbelieving father at his weakest. But then I looked at Mom, who folded her hands in her lap and prayed earnestly, eyes closed, and I forgave him.

Bruce, who had arrived just minutes before, stood with his arms dangling and looked at the floor. Behind his slightly impatient gaze was the memory, I suspected, of what he'd written in his book about the last time a Lutheran pastor had suggested praying over our father. Dad had been on the verge of death, we thought, on his way out of his and Mom's living room on a gurney. The pastor, who had come in response to Mom's call, had asked Dad if he could put him on the congregation's prayer tree. Dad, even though he was barely able to breathe, had refused, saying that, having never been a church man, he didn't want to be a hypocrite. This is the exchange the way my brother wrote it:

"We're all hypocrites. That's why we do pray," said the preacher.

"Well, I'm not," said Harold. "That's why I don't."

"I didn't say that," my father told Bruce when he first read the book. Bruce insisted he did.

On this particular morning, the pastor put in a worthy request—that our family would find the strength to hold together through trying times.

When it was over, Dad said, "Well, sometimes I wish the man would listen better." I found this remark amusing and could see from Bruce's grin that he did too. "The man" Dad referred to wasn't God, but his foreman, Ron. With the exception of the weather, Dad recognized no powers other than those belonging to himself and the other men he knew.

I glance south, where Ron is turning his rig to begin another pass through the pintos. Is he cultivating them? I'm not even sure. I can only pray that he understands this enterprise well enough to manage it. Yes, I think I'd better pray. That and try to fire up my inner computer. I remember the way Dad sprayed highly combustible ether in the carburetors of tractors on cold mornings. Maybe his death will shock the farmer awake in me.

I helped plant this crop in September. Seeing this day coming and aware of my congenital inability to pay attention through the mind-numbing tractor rounds, I took notes in my writing journal on planting rates and everything else that might prove important. The varieties. Tam 107 on dryland, Ike or Carl on irrigated. Where the hidden zerks were on the drill. What joint grass seed looked like and a reminder to watch for it as I loaded the drill's planter boxes. All the equipment's anomalies—how the gas gauge on the John Deere 4630 registered a quarter tank when it was actually empty, a fact I learned the hard way; the differing functions of the power take off levers on the seed trucks; and how if you touched the ungrounded switch on the auger motor of the old red truck, you'd get a 110 volt shock. These and a hundred other things.

During that planting season, I watched my father with the increasing appreciation a child feels only as her parents age. I marveled over how he could dig behind a drill's press wheel and uncover a seed, which I could never do though I dug a trench six feet long. With my aid, my father lowered himself onto the ground and perched on his hands and knees in a humbling position that spoke volumes of our real relation to the earth. He scooped away a handful of the top, dry dirt, then flicked with the handle of his open pliers in the narrow groove carved by the drill's seed spout. A pale kernel showed itself, a tiny vulva, destined to open soon in birth. My father, an unlikely midwife, brushed away the remaining flecks of dirt with his huge index finger. "See there," he said. The secret of good wheat, he reminded me, was to plant as shallow as possible, to position the seed just barely in the moisture.

I am struck as I scan the surrounding fields by the brilliance of all the trucks and wheat—red and gold beneath a satin sky, royal colors. That spirit of fanfare infiltrates the conversations you hear in every store and restaurant near harvesttime. Not just the bottom line, *What's it makin'?* but the other, supporting details.

The tare's no more'n one percent. We're cuttin' clean.

It was testing thirteen this morning. Still too wet to cut.

The men and the men-kids, be they male or female, never get over the huge combines. They drive them all day, but the pride still roils in them as they crest a rise or enter a new field.

Most of them would say they are Christians, but, like my father, they really worship the machines. All the lights and computer technology, the mammoth dimensions. Even the huge, tandem-axle trucks seem to pay obeisance to the combines, often following along beside them in the field, loading on the go. These machines and our science—the way we prime the ground with fertilizers and spray the young crops with chemicals—make us think that we do it all. This recurring miracle for which we take the credit defines us as a people, and we tune to it, as if humming an old ballad. Wheat is the measure of us, in bushels. If we're good farmers—steadfast, worthy—the yields are high.

My father was a good farmer, but was quick to point out that staying in the business also required caution. He was a financial conservative who refrained from borrowing money. More than once he'd seen neighbors "lose their ass and all the plumbing" because they mortgaged their land to expand. He also refrained from placing too much faith in one crop. Besides his wheat and irrigated crops, he raised livestock. During the last several years he ran cattle, but for most of his life he was a "sheepman," his self-designation. His one thousand ewes and, every spring, their twelve hundred lambs, were more labor intensive than cattle, but also more profitable. When grain markets dropped, the markets for spring lambs and wool held steady.

He dreamed about sheep the night before he died. I stole into the hospital and sat in his darkened room as the nurses' shoes squeaked past on the hall's shiny tile. He was sleeping propped up, a common display, through those many doorways, of age and illness. His sleep didn't require privacy. It just asserted itself the way the final pall would one night later, when I would be sleeping peacefully back in my bed in Laramie, thinking he was pulling through yet another crisis.

I dragged the chair close to the bed.

He started, grunted, opened his eyes. The glasses we'd brought him earlier lay where we'd left them, on top of the *Denver Post*. Now, he looked at me vacantly, no light coming into his eyes. I had a moment's uncertainty. Was I a nearly forgotten entity or a given? Forgotten due to my abandonment of him ten years earlier, when I opted for a writing and teaching career over farming, or honored with the complacency reserved for family? He coughed, knit his brows, winced. "I must have fallen asleep," he said, as if this were unexpected and a little irresponsible of him.

"Go right ahead. I just wanted to look in on you."

He complied, easing his bald head back on the pillow, his eyes falling shut. He slept fitfully for awhile, then woke and looked dully at me. "Been raining out?"

I told him it hadn't. "Do you think the wheat's been harmed much by the drought?" I asked, but Dad's eyes had closed again. I let the minutes slip by, the air in the room brimming with a knowledge that we were not givens to each other, that the only true given was death. I knew I couldn't bear what I was going to have to bear. I couldn't just watch him slip off into the night. At the same time, I wanted to be there when it happened. I vowed to be a very attentive daughter. We all knew he was dying. Knew it in the intellectual sense, although it wasn't really comprehensible. We expected it to take several months, and I thought this night was just one of many during which I would sit by his bed, not the last.

My meditations were interrupted by a sudden announcement from Dad. "I didn't know Bruce sold his sheep."

I leaned forward. "What did you say?"

His eyes were still closed, but his jaw was chewing, as if on the pleasure of his words and what they indicated. A son carrying on. "Well, Bruce still wants to run sheep."

I grabbed an ATM withdrawal slip from my wallet, the only thing I had to write on, and scribbled down his next words, leaving out the phrases that were unintelligible. "Well, a lot better ... in this industry.... A sheepman, you bring in...." In an essay I had once described his voice as "whiskery." Another time I had said it was full of road gravel. His tone, as usual, was a

familiar one, explanatory, authoritative. Did Dad envision his
living room, his feet slung out on the recliner rest, and I across
from him in the turquoise rocker, the supplicant's chair? I liked
to think I was at least part of the dream, if not the leading topic
of interest.

"Well, you see," he continued. "They'll steal others' brands.
So simple to change a ewe's number. But when a little lamb'll
bring one hundred twenty-five dollars, it's time to sell."
Someone, he added, although I didn't catch the name, "gets a
lot of cattle bred in the fall."

A voice came over the PA, announcing that visiting hours
were over. It surprised me to discover I'd been there legally all
along. Dad opened his eyes, which were mystified.

"Dad? I'm leaving now." I squeezed his foot through the
thin white blanket. "You going to be warm enough?"

"You're leaving?"

"Did you know you've been talking in your sleep?"

"I have?"

"You had Bruce back in the sheep business. He sold, but it
was okay. You said that with market lambs so high, it was time
to sell."

"Somehow my mind always comes back to money." This
was the family joke about him, and he'd always played along,
willing to take the brunt of our humor. But his voice was flat
now, his lungs and heart too weak for inflection, the statement
sounding rueful, as though he were disappointed in himself.

I stole out of the hospital richer than when I'd stolen into
it. My father's dreams didn't surprise or disappoint me. He was
a man whose passions ran to bone.

I stand up and brush the dirt from my jeans. It
has occurred to me that it is really pointless to wait for Jake to
come back. As my deceased father has pointed out, I won't be
seeing him for a long time. Allowed to, he would ride with
Jessica well past nightfall, when the dinosaurs' halogen eyes

rove the fields, causing the wheat to glow moon-pale.

It is always the wheat I come back to. Twelve dollars for every acre, twelve cents for every bushel hauled, and twelve cents for every bushel over twenty per acre. *That's it!* I can feel the numbers mounting in me, the columns of figures setting up camp in my brain. But it is the more basic equation that amazes me—from bare ground and fall tedium to this orgy of plenty every summer. Dad was not a reverent man, but I know we all felt things as the truck beds brimmed that neither his pragmatism nor Mom's religion gave us the means to express. By rights, it is the wheat that my people should worship. We should cut our inner arms, fill chalices with blood and sprinkle it over each field in gratitude for how the wheat gives itself, how it comes back to us year after year, how the seed sown into bare ground has never failed to yield fruit.

"Yet!" my skeptical father would say, making a pronouncement of his doubt over benevolence in the universe. "It hasn't failed yet."

The Tossed Purse

Since my father's death, two years ago, my mother visits me occasionally here in Laramie. Last summer I took her to the Fourth of July celebration in Washington Park. We sat on the grass and ate ice-cream cones handed out by the old men of the American Legion. When it came time to stand back up, Mom said, "Now let me just try this by myself. I need to learn." She had broken her hip the year before, and, just as my father had retrained his mind after a stroke by reciting the capitols of the fifty states, she had been working on regaining full use of her leg.

I reached down and picked up her handbag, then stood in my jeans and faded T-shirt while my frail mother, in her apricot knit slacks and vest and her floral print blouse with the bow at the neck, tried to raise herself off the ground. She got up on her hands and knees and grunted, saying "Ooh, ooh my." One of the Legionnaires dashed over and offered her his hand, which she accepted graciously. I could feel the onlookers' recriminating stares. *She didn't want my help,* I wished to explain to them.

I admired my mother's desire to be self-reliant and had seen her get up by herself before. While waiting, I'd drifted off, contemplating the awkward heft of her purse on my arm. I barely waited for my mother to dust the grass from her slacks before restoring the bag to its home on her arm. Considering my haste, it might have been a bodily organ, throbbing with life that could not go on for long, exposed to open air.

I recall this moment because of a dream I had a month after her visit, while I was attending a writers' conference in central Vermont, where greenery formed a tangle all the way to the ground. Originally a plainswoman and now a westerner, I'm accustomed to greater spaciousness, and it seems only natural that my unconscious returned me to my mother's and my original home, our farmhouse on the High Plains of western Kansas, where we both grew up.

I was a child in the dream, which opened in a blur of confused action inside my brother Bruce's second-story bedroom. Other kids shuffled about me, fighting, or just playing hard. I held my purse above the fray, then, spotting an open window, tossed it out.

A sudden change of scene, and I was walking, as an adult, out a door onto a cement stoop that was perhaps six by eight feet, and not very high. Beyond the stoop, in the dirt, lay a black, rectangular purse. It was clearly empty, its sides flat. *How odd*, I thought, *a purse, here*, but, remembering the window in my brother's room, became aware that "here" was the back step of our farmhouse.

I could feel the door at my back. It gave entrance not only to a flight of stairs leading up into the kitchen, but to another flight leading down into the black basement. The basement had both frightened and enticed me as a child. I dream of it often, to this day. I have talked with my dead brother Clark in that basement, and once witnessed a procession of women going over the stoop and down the stairs. The women were my deceased aunts, all in housedresses, and leading them was my grandmother Carlson, she of the cantankerous temperament and sagging, aged flesh and nubbin bun, she who died when I was only nine. She wore one of her shapeless, cap-sleeved acetate dresses, white with navy polka dots. My mother fell right into place and followed without looking to either side, while I stood at an angle to the women, off the edge of the stoop. As if I were a witness merely. As if I didn't belong among them. But they marched inexorably, my membership unquestioned, inevitable.

Now, beyond that same stoop, the empty, unadorned purse lay perfectly square with the edge of the concrete, as if it had been placed there purposefully, rather than dropped from an open window.

Another sudden change of scene took me outside the fence, at the northwest corner of the yard. I pushed the wire down with my hand and stepped over it into a drab world, the entire house yard turned to rubble. I stood beside a pile of broken, soot-bruised bricks that used to be our incinerator. All was gray, gone. All was lost. There was no house, only a few low cement pillars, the kind that might provide bases for statues, but there were no statues. The mulberry trees that had bordered the yard on the north were dead, their trunks jagged amidst their own fallen limbs. Grief overwhelmed me. Facing southeast, where the house once reigned over the plains, I buckled at the middle and hugged myself in the manner of an anguished little girl. "Mommy!" I called instinctively. The shout caused me to rise, extending my arms slightly behind me. "Mommy!" I called, against hope.

Behind me and to my right, chickens began clucking. The sound made it seem as if the huge prairie sky spanned a concert hall, and resonant within it, stringed instruments had begun tuning, discordant, hopeful. Looking around me, I saw that the chickens drifted through both the house and hog yard, filling the space, populating it with life. They strutted as they pecked, stepped, pecked, beaks bobbing for seed, their red combs flopping.

My chest and stomach, depleted by my shouts, filled again with air. "Daddy!" I shouted, drawing the syllables out with more hope now than desperation. Light rose all around me, as, in some hidden control room, a technician, fingers spread, slid an entire panel of dimmers upward. Beyond the east fence on the opposite side of the yard, sun glinted off a huge, corrugated tin building, the sheep barn from our other farm, where my father had consolidated his holdings after we moved to town. Just then, in the parallel universe of wakefulness beyond the theater doors, a dorm mate picked up the hall phone. She began to speak in what seemed to me, as I woke, the most irritating of voices about the most crass of concerns, subverting the return of my relatives. I had thought if I kept shouting I could have it all back, our lost life on that farm.

My grief among the dream rubble, then the welcome appearance of the chickens and barn, overshadowed the purse. I would have forgotten it entirely were it not for a friend I'd made at the conference. Both in our fifties, she and I discussed our attempts to invent lives that fulfill us while also seeking continuity with our pasts.

"I think your dream is about your mother," my friend said. "Just ask yourself, who tends chickens, and what do they produce?" Chickens symbolized fertility, motherhood, the giving and protecting of life. Suggesting I needed to get in touch with my "feminine side," she encouraged me to write about my mother.

"I will," I said. "Someday."

I didn't need my friend's knowing look to tell me my answer was a dodge. "The purse is the most female image going!" she added, trying to get me to heed my own unconscious. "In psychoanalytic dream theory, it represents the womb."

If I am out of touch with my feminine side, it is probably because the concept of femininity, as I absorbed it growing up, came to me laden in paradox. As a girl, I learned to feel shame over my approaching womanhood, even if ads in teen magazines did assure me that the perfectly designed sanitary pad or tampon would allow me to continue projecting a virginal purity, as I did pirouettes in my white leotard and soft-pink tutu. My mother, like most other women I knew, treated menstruation as if it were a dark secret, a curse. Womanhood seemed a project in concealment, denial, and fiction. She herself had two personae, one for home and one for town. At home, she wore everyday housedresses, faded from many washings. Because her parents had put her in shoes too small for her as a child, her toes curled under and she suffered from corns. Mornings, she pulled on thin white anklets and black orthopedic lace-ups. They had a wide, two-inch heel. Wrapping her varicose veins in an Ace bandage, she often explained that flats hurt her calves. She had a bit of a belly, quite normal in a woman who had borne three children, but when she went to town, she pulled on a girdle and adopted the glamorous look of the women we saw in new car ads in Life magazine and Saturday Evening Post.

Before stepping into one of her beautiful wool suits and lowering a matching hat over her freshly curled hair, she guided silk stockings over her deformed toes and over her shapely, although aching, calves. She adjusted the black back seams in her dresser mirror and eased her feet into one of her many pairs of gorgeous high heels. In the fifties the toes of these pumps were round and sophisticated. In the sixties they ended in a point sharp enough to burst a balloon. My mother wore them all. She disguised the pain well, but couldn't walk as fast as my father. Looking dapper in his wool pants and his town fedora with the orange feather in the band, he would forget himself at times and stride ahead of her. "Slow down, Harold. I can't keep up," Mom would say, a bit of her mother's complaining drawl surfacing in her voice. Holding my father's hand as we walked, I could feel his irritation. He was used to covering distance on the farm, and it was hard for him to reduce his long stride. Feeling a little surge of Oedipal pride, I noted that I could keep up with him just fine.

That spurned purse was black, I suspect, for a reason. It rested at that back door, through which my dead aunts, led by my dead grandmother, had disappeared. When I tossed it out, I was young. When I rediscovered it, I was fifty. My mother is now eighty. When I left home with my first husband, I spared her scarcely a backward glance, and it seemed she let go of me just as easily. She sent me off in the manner of plainspeople, who believe that grown children should have their own lives. Her letters didn't inquire about my happiness, but focused on the weather back home, the state of her garden, the success of Dad's crops. When I divorced that man, she didn't ask me why.

The one insight I've had into my mother's silence came in reaction to an essay I once wrote called "At Forty-five." In it, I noted her reticence on personal topics. I sent her the essay in advance of its publication in a national newspaper. I didn't want her to hear about it by happenstance. Happily, she wasn't offended. My love announced itself in the piece with enough clarity to flatter her, and breaking that emotional silence for the first time ever, she wrote to me saying the reason she didn't discuss personal issues rested in her fear that doing so would cause her to cry. Her mother had always told her that "good little Indians" didn't cry.

I'd been stifled by the same fear. Conversation among women when I was a child resembled dressing for town in the fifties and early sixties, when we poured ourselves into preformed undergarments. Don't say anything if you can't say anything nice.

As a child, I didn't like it when my mother violated the rigid code against weakness and issued one of her physical complaints. "I think I might skip eating tonight. My stomach's been bothering me all day," she would say as she laid platters of food on the table. She would repeat herself as she sat down. "I don't know if I can eat anything. My stomach's upset. I've always had a nervous stomach." I would set my jaw and resist granting her the small bit of attention she must have craved.

Today, I am a little more ready to offer sympathy, while she is little less likely to ask for it. She seldom complains of physical ailments anymore. When she broke her hip a year after my father's death, she went through the recovery in high spirits. When I complimented her, she said, "I took a lesson from your father. You know, it was terrible for him to be laid up like that.

Imagine! A man of his energy! But he never showed his frustration. He never got angry with me. He was patient, and always so pleasant."

I am hopeful that she will one day feel free to discuss the more fundamental grievances that her physical complaints might have camouflaged. "What are the things you can't talk about without crying?" I asked her over the phone after I received her letter.

"Oh, there isn't anything that bothers me particularly much. It's just the way I am."

"It's the way I am too, but there's no shame in a few tears. We need the release sometimes."

Silence on her end of the line.

"Know what I mean?"

"Oh yes, sure," she said, drifting back in.

How to begin, then? Any genuine question seems an invasion of my mother's long, well-maintained privacy. I wish most to ask her about my brother Clark, not just to assuage our grief, but because, as a mother of only one child myself, her loss strikes terror in my heart. I need to probe that fear, but I have managed to say only a few things.

"Remember that last Christmas we had together, when he, the kids, and I formed a choo-choo train and bounced down the stairs on our butts?"

"Yes," Mom said, her tone lifting with the memory.

"He pulled Jake through the snow that Christmas vacation too. He tied a rope to the sled and pretended to be a reindeer. He said he didn't know what sound a reindeer made, so he whinnied like a horse."

Mom's eyes grew distant as I recited the details. She nodded and murmured assent. Was she seeing Clark in his green and black Lycra jogging suit, ice dangling from his mustache? Was she remembering, as I did, how out of place he looked dressed that way in Kansas? Was she wondering, as I often do, if we'd done enough to demonstrate we loved him even though the world had changed him? Had he *ever* known how loved he was?

I can't think of that Christmas without also remembering Clark shoveling the drive with Bruce. Bruce grabbed his chest and fell over in a snowbank, pretending to have a heart attack. I can still laugh at that memory, but am not sure Mom could.

"Clark would have meant so much to Jake by now," I've said.

"Yes, he would have."

I once told Mom my dreams of Clark, saying they seem to prove that at least something goes on. "I've always known that," Mom said, the stress underscoring my heathenism.

I want to ask her, *How did you manage to go on living? Was it because you have other children? What if you hadn't?* I want to console her and share my own fear.

Getting to that point seems possible, but it will take work, and time that I'm not sure we have. We are gradually gaining an appreciation of each other that our focus on Dad didn't allow. I feel a creature warmth when she's near that derives from our shared past on the farm. Life, in its many odd and surprising permutations, fascinated her. "Look at that worm!" she would shout in her garden, using a twig to peel a green-spotted, horned monster off one of her tomato plants. "Where do they come from? Where?" Her stories, to this day, are populated by the animals she has known—our dog Flopsy, who nursed an orphaned kitten we named Freak; the pet toad who would sit with Mom and her siblings on the east porch stoop summer nights, gorging on June bugs; Joe the Crow, who chased the dogs and cats away and ate their food; the ducks who disappeared in a blizzard and came back a week later. "Just quacking to beat the band. If only they could talk. Where do you suppose they had been?"

My mother enjoyed her most recent visit here in Laramie more than any other. After six years here, I've made some good friends, some of whom joined us for meals, and it was the annual Jubilee Days celebration. Each day, Mom dressed in one of the brightly colored knit pantsuits she had made herself, laced up her best orthopedic shoes (which have only a slight lift in the heel—she wears high heels no longer), tie a scarf over her hair, and go with me to a different event. We took in the Freedom Has a Birthday celebration in Washington Park, attended the fireworks and concert at the University football stadium, and went to a potluck at a friend's house. I hadn't seen her laugh so hard in years, not since the aunts and uncles used to gather round our holiday table. Afterwards, she said, repeatedly, "You have such wonderful friends!"

I even got Mom to drive up in the mountains with me and a girlfriend, who took us to an alpine meadow she camps in. We traveled miles of jeep trail in this friend's four-wheel-drive van, fording a stream at one point. Mom spent most of her life in the country, but she and Dad never strayed off the highway when visiting the mountains. She was frightened, but also enchanted by our wilderness adventure, and it cheered me to be showing her, finally, the kind of country my spirit thrives on—although she made me promise, falsely, that I would never tow my horse up there.

Mom was amazed during that visit by simple things—the thunder in the stadium as the crowd thumped their feet to welcome the lead singing act, the gulls that had swooped overhead as the sun set behind us, the bawling of a cow in the meadow where I helped my friend put up the tent she planned to leave there all summer. Witnessing these things, Mom's face took on an almost childish wonder. Her mouth hung open a bit, lips parted, white teeth shining. Her eyes seemed bluer than ever, her skin translucent. One friend, who had only read about my mother in my essays, was surprised by a quality she called "ethereal," and I had to agree. This quality had appeared in my mother recently. To my relief, she had stopped tinting her hair blond. It had grown out a shimmering gold-lit silver, much like my hair, which my father often told me I should color. "Harold always rode me about the gray," she informed me. "He would let me know the minute he saw the roots showing. But gee, I've been getting lots of compliments on it. I'm going to leave it this way."

While the conversations I wish to have with my mother still seem a long way off, I try to reconcile myself. Perhaps what we have is enough. Perhaps we will enter on a pleasant, unanalyzed cohabitation. I have thought of moving her up here when she gets too old to navigate her house alone. But I know our days would be filled with frustrating ships-in-the-night dialogue like the one we had after that last visit.

I was taking her to Denver, where she would catch a plane the rest of the way to Goodland. Loading the car, I told her, "You're pretty brave, Mom, to be flying alone."

"Why thank you. There's no reason you should have to drive all that way."

Several blocks of good feeling silence ensued, during which I turned on NPR. The news informed us that President Clinton had been visiting various poor communities around the country. He'd given a speech at the Pine Ridge Indian Reservation.

"You know one thing I don't understand?" Mom said.

I reached over and turned down the radio's volume, which I'd had on high because she wasn't wearing her hearing aid. "What?"

"What is wrong with those Indians? Everyone always says they can't make it like we can. Well, why not?"

"Pine Ridge, Mom? That's only a little over two hundred miles north of Goodland, in South Dakota. The massacre that took place there was in one of those books I gave Dad. *Old Jules,* by Mari Sandoz. He read it, I know, and we talked about it," I said, calling on my father's absent authority to shore up my point. "I mean we did that everywhere, just went in and wiped them out, men, women, children."

"I know things like that happened. Our church contributes to the Indians all the time. But why *do* they still have so much trouble?"

I shrugged and sighed. It seemed ironic that my grandmother had called on Indian stoicism to keep her children in
line. "We didn't just wipe out their ancestors, we wiped out
their whole way of life!" I laid my hand out palm up, underscoring my frustration.

We went several miles in silence, listening to the radio. The
news gave way to folk music and light rock, and I felt our
moods improving. "Isn't it amazing?" I said, gesturing at the
mountain range we were passing.

"It sure is," she said, staring in the direction where we'd
had our little adventure only a few days before. "Can I ask you
a personal question?"

"Of course!" The notion of my mother asking me something personal thrilled me.

"When you're out there in the middle of nowhere like that,
what do you do about going to the bathroom?"

"Gee, Mom. It's no big problem. Just go. Haven't you ever
squatted in a field?"

"Well, yes, but I want some privacy for things like that."

"It's not like anyone would be watching. We were alone in
a million acres of wilderness!"

As we neared Fort Collins, the first city on our route to
Denver, I noticed here and there a new house—up on a ridge,
or wedged in a canyon. Of all the terrible things that were happening in the West, the loss of open space disturbed me more
than anything else. Someone had built a particularly ostenta-
tious three-story house in a vast meadow.

"Now there's a beautiful house," Mom said.

"I hate it, though, when people plunk their houses down in
the middle of a sweeping vista, as if they owned it all. They ruin
it for everyone else."

"Well, they own the land. They've got to put their house
somewhere."

I drove the remaining miles into Fort Collins in silence,
wondering if our differences frustrated my mother as much as

they did me. I peed in the wilderness, went downtown in jeans, didn't carry a handbag, held views on land ownership more in keeping with the attitudes of the Indians, whose plight mystified her. At the potluck, a friend had joked with us, saying, boy, he could tell her stories about me. "No don't," was my mother's well-considered answer. "I think I'd rather not hear."

I suspect that my mother is battle scarred, from the sixties. Her policy of not asking and not wanting to know is due not only to Plains stoicism, but to a self-protective instinct that kicked in when she launched her children out into that pandemonium. Clark had missed the sixties mostly, but the younger Bruce and I had both experimented with drugs. My first husband, like Bruce, had grown his hair long and worn a beard. This seemingly benign choice had been a rebellious pronouncement in the generational war. Then there had been our divorces, which were not just breaks with our partners, but with the way things were and should be. Bruce redeemed himself by staying married to his second wife and having two kids with her. Mom got in the habit of believing that any news from my quarter would be disturbing.

"Ah, here we are," she said, as we came to the first stoplight.

"Yes, here's Fort Collins."

"Harold went to school here."

"He had some high times here," I said, hating how few of the actual details from my father's stories I remembered. I looked around the downtown area, wondering which of the buildings he had helped dig a foundation for. They did it with shovels and wheelbarrows in those days, he'd said, and the pay was phenomenally small. With that pittance, he bought his books, paid his rent in the rooming house, fed himself poorly—on what I couldn't remember.

Several blocks passed under us, with many stops and starts at lights. "You know," Mom said, her tone amazed as she recognized the downtown area. "I believe I came here all by myself once."

"You did?"

"Yes I did," she said proudly. "It was for a church meeting of some kind. I drove up here all by myself."

"Did you stay in a hotel?"

She thought for a few seconds. "No, I don't think so. I stayed with some people who were members of the church here."

"Did you ever do that any other time—drive somewhere? Alone?" I heard myself ask this tenderly.

"Oh yes, I used to do all sorts of things," she said, unaware of the contrast she was drawing, inadvertently, between her life and mine. "I drove to Lindsborg, Kansas once, with two other church women. That town was founded by Swedes, and they had this wonderful smorgasbord restaurant. That was for a Make It Yourself With Wool contest. I went all over the place when I was president of that. Rosie and I went to Salina by ourselves, and then one time your dad and I flew all the way down to Mexico City for a Wool Growers meeting!"

What would my mother have done, I wondered, if Dad had died when she was much younger? I thought it likely that she would have met another man, at church probably. In her day-dreams she might picture me wearing one of the frilly blouses she sometimes buys me for Christmas, joining a church in Laramie, and doing that myself.

Thank God for my father. He spared me a life full of churched niceness. Or should I thank the Devil? Mom went over to the wild a bit herself by marrying Dad. In my ongoing effort to communicate, I asked her in a recent telephone conversation why she did marry my father, knowing he lacked religion, and she replied with the force of the obvious.

"Because I loved the so and so! Haven't you seen those pictures of him when he was a young man? He was beautiful!"

"Did you think you could convert him?"

"Oh, I tried to get him to go to church. My mother tried too, but he wouldn't budge. He believed in science, and he just couldn't get religion."

"But did it bother you?"

"No, not really," she said thoughtfully. "You know, I've always been kind of a doubter myself."

We'd been on opposite sides of this fence so long that I'd forgotten her admissions of as much in the distant past. In trying to understand our differences, I categorize too often, sorting them into dualities.

There have been other crossovers that attest to our being members of the same faith, so to speak. Mom and Dad both came over to my brothers' and my side on Vietnam. Mom led the way in that conversion. "I don't know what business we've got, sticking our noses in other people's affairs like that. And then having our own boys dying. For what?" she nearly shouted, thinking no doubt of my brothers. "Our own boys!" Nixon was the last Republican my mother ever voted for, and Dad stopped voting a straight ticket because of her. They jumped the fence as easily on this as Mom's chickens did, in my dream.

Those chickens drifted over the ground inside and outside the yard. I'd seen how they crossed many times as a child. When they felt like it, they just hopped over, or squeezed through the rectangles in the hog wire. They were oblivious to the separation of house and field. Remembering this I find both instructive and freeing, since that barrier between genders was impenetrable in the minds of my mother and father.

I remember vividly the joy I felt, hearing the chickens clucking behind me in my dream. How grateful I was for that reemergence of life in the context of bleak, deathly loss. My friend from the conference has written me, adding that the appearance of my father's sheep barn, accompanied by rising light, might indicate the dream was sent to me by someone on the other side. "Someone who must care about you very much," she wrote. I burst into tears reading her letter, so great is my longing for my father. How wonderful it would be if my atheist dad is now reaching over to assure me, from that "other side." Yet, as grateful as I was for that sign, whether of or from him, the chickens were the breakthrough. They came in response to my first call, for my mother. That was the miracle. Through dreaming, I discovered a need I'd long denied.

My mother and I are making progress. We are asking questions, demonstrating a willingness to consider each other's realities and to recognize each other's successes. She would not have asked that "private" question about the forest if she were still completely embedded in her fearful, sixties mode. She was allowing herself to imagine what it would be like to camp up there. We'd been to Fort Collins many times before, but this was the first time she'd reminisced over her solitary car trip.

Maybe, if I keep shouting long enough and hard enough, we'll start asking the hard questions, the ones that risk tears. Maybe I'll be able to tell her I know she possesses much that I lack—the security of having lived within a balanced universe, the rows in her garden aligned perfectly with the straight rows in my father's field, beyond the fence; a good marriage that I insist she made good by subsuming herself, but she apparently didn't notice the sacrifice.

Why, in the dream, did I call out for her first? Because she is the one remaining, the only avenue to completeness? Or could it be that this is the natural order, to which I'm able to return only now, with Dad gone? It was always his lap I wanted to sit in, his work I aspired to, his eyes I hoped to make shine. I have told my dream to others, who have objected to my friend's deployment of the womb symbol. One friend suggested that my tossing the purse stood for my financial independence. Sometimes a purse is just a purse, said another acquaintance. But no purse is just a purse in the lexicon of either my waking or sleeping consciousness and, while the wallets inside them might signify finances, in my hand or bulging on my hip a purse implies an acceptance of the adjectives that hovered over me as I was growing up. Girls were slower, dumber, weaker than boys.

I didn't just happen to be in my brother's room when the dream opened. I abandoned Mom's side of the gender divide in an attempt to gain equality with Bruce. I tossed the purse out the window because it handicapped me in the competition that raged between us over our father's love.

My mother is doing surprisingly well on her own. Surprisingly well for a woman whose daughter has always believed she lived through her husband. She has her club and church meetings. She volunteers, still, every Wednesday afternoon at the Good Samaritan Center, a retirement home where she leads the "old people" in Bingo. She's older than many of them now. She expects to wind up there herself someday, but I have trouble countenancing that. She could come live with me, I tell her. Unless she thinks she'd be happier in Goodland, where she has friends? I receive the customary evasion. "Well, I don't know." Our conversations often drift off this way.

This doesn't bother her the way it does me. She doesn't seem to get unbearably lonely either, not as lonely as I do, in fact. And noticing this, I am reminded that, no matter how liberated I think I am in comparison to her, I have not had all the luck. She still lives, through the habit of memory, in that balanced universe I screamed out for, in my dream. Her ethereal quality comes not just from the natural silver and gold highlights in her hair, but the contentment she feels remembering her life with that good-looking so and so, my father. Because of that, home goes where she goes and makes my own home, when she's in it, more complete.

"If there's a penny to pinch, she'll find it," my father used to brag about my thrifty mother. She can't stand to see a dime turned away for naught, and so I enticed her to come up for her first visit by kicking out my renter and joking with her over the phone, telling her that I'd turned the space into the Jasmin Bair Commemorative Guest Room. I bought her a reading chair. Next, I think I'll install a light over it and get rid of the desk lamp that sits on the side table now and is difficult to aim right. I've been thinking seriously about a renovation that might make her room seem more inviting still. I plan to knock out a good portion of the south wall and put in a bay window like the one that used to let in so much light, on the farm.

Acknowledgments

I wish to thank Carl Klaus, who, as Director of the Nonfiction Writing Program at the University of Iowa, introduced me to the personal essay. My deepest gratitude also to Jo Ann Beard and Patricia Stevens, writing friends who lent their wisdom, generosity, and talent to the reading of many drafts of these essays over the years. I am deeply indebted to many others in my literary community, past and present. They are Garry Alkire, Clark Blaise, Barbara Camillo, Liz Carpenter, Marian Clark, Bryan Costales, Susan Davis, Laura Dowd, Patricia Foster, Karol Griffin, Linda Hasselstrom, Will Jennings, Diane Kaufman, Sheryl Lain, Lisa Dale Norton, C. L. Rawlins, Mike Shay, Michael Steinberg, Shirley Tarbell, my agent Elyse Cheney, and the dedicated, gifted critics and writers of the Silver Sage Writers Alliance. Thanks to the organizers of the Bread Loaf Conference and to Neltje and the Wyoming Arts Council for encouraging me with their notice, and thanks also to Deb Clow and Don Snow, whose journal, *Northern Lights*, grants western literary writers an elegant venue. I am profoundly grateful to Elizabeth Mische for applying her keen ear and discernment, and to Marianne Nora and Lane Stiles of Mid-List Press for honoring my work with their fine editing and publishing talents. I thank my mother, son, brother, and cousins for enduring my imperfect renditions, and for their support and love.